The Learning Portfolio

The Learning Portfolio

*Reflective Practice for
Improving Student Learning*

John Zubizarreta
Columbia College

ANKER PUBLISHING COMPANY, INC.
Bolton, Massachusetts

The Learning Portfolio
Reflective Practice for Improving Student Learning

IBSN 1-882982-66-5

Composition by Deerfoot Studios
Cover design by Jennifer Arbaiza Graphic Design

Anker Publishing Company, Inc.
176 Ballville Road
P. O. Box 249
Bolton, MA 01740-0249

www.ankerpub.com

About the Author

John Zubizarreta is professor of English and director of honors and faculty development at Columbia College, South Carolina. A Carnegie Foundation/Council for the Advancement and Support of Education Professor of the Year for South Carolina, he has also earned awards and recognition for teaching and scholarly excellence from the American Association for Higher Education, the South Atlantic Association of Departments of English, the National United Methodist Board of Higher Education, the South Carolina Commission on Higher Education, and other educational organizations.

John is a frequent conference presenter and consultant on improving college teaching, learning, and academic leadership, and he has mentored educators nationwide and internationally on developing teaching and administrative portfolios. His work on portfolios—often in collaboration with Peter Seldin—includes many articles and chapters in journal and book publications such as *The Journal on Excellence in College Teaching; The Department Chair; Phi Delta Kappan;* Seldin's *Changing Practices in Evaluating Teaching* (1999), *The Teaching Portfolio, Second Edition* (1997), *Improving College Teaching* (1995), *Successful Use of Teaching Portfolios* (1993); Roth's *Inspiring Teaching* (1997); and Wright's *Teaching Improvement Practices* (1995). He also has contributed to Seldin and Higgerson's *The Administrative Portfolio* (2002).

In addition to his scholarly work on teaching and learning, John has published widely on modern American and comparative literatures. Foremost among his disciplinary publications is his co-edited *Robert Frost Encyclopedia* (2001).

John is also a devoted husband and father of two girls. When the academic life becomes too hectic, John is an avid telemark skier and fisherman, an aching runner, and a former six-time gold medalist champion in national whitewater canoe competition.

About the Contributors

Tanya Augsburg is a performance scholar who teaches in the Bachelor of Interdisciplinary Studies Program at Arizona State University. She lectures and writes on the growing use of portfolios for personal, educational, and professional development, and she is currently working on a volume on contemporary performance and an introductory textbook on interdisciplinary studies.

Lisa Batterbee is director of user services at Albion College, where she works in the fields of residential life and information technology. She has been digital portfolio coordinator since Albion began its Digital Portfolio Project. Her master's degree is from Central Michigan University.

Vicki Bocchicchio is coordinator of curriculum and faculty development for the Honors College at Kent State University, where she is also a Ph.D. student in the literature program.

David G. Brown is vice president, professor of economics, and dean of the International Center for Computer-Enhanced Learning at Wake Forest University. He has served as president of Transylvania University; chancellor of the University of North Carolina, Asheville; provost at three universities (Wake Forest, Miami of Ohio, and Drake); and chaired several national groups including the American Association for Higher Education, Higher Education Colloquium, the American Council on Education's Council of Chief Academic Officers, and the National Association of State Universities and Land-Grant Colleges' Academic Council.

Earl B. Brown, Jr. is professor of English and served as honors director at Radford University for 13 years. During that time, he developed a program widely recognized for its innovative approaches to honors education.

Jená A. Burges directs both the general education and freshman writing programs at Longwood College. Formerly a high school English teacher on the edge of the Navajo Nation, she now teaches courses in composition, writing pedagogy, grammar, and linguistics. Her research interests include writing pedagogy and assessment, interdisciplinary learning, and organizational and public discourse.

Candee C. Chambers earned her doctorate in chemistry in 1994 at Oklahoma State University. Her research was in the area of theoretical physical chemistry. Currently, she is associate professor of physics and chemistry and director of the Honors Program at Mercyhurst College.

Andrew Dunham is assistant dean for the First-Year Experience and former assistant dean of students and director of Campus Programs and Organizations at Albion College. He has degrees in music and a Ph.D. in college student personnel administration.

L. Dee Fink has served as director of the Instructional Development Program at the University of Oklahoma for 23 years. Active nationally in the Professional and Organizational Development Network in Higher Education, he is the author of *Creating Significant Learning Experiences in College Classrooms: An Integrated Approach to Designing College Courses* (2003).

Eileen Herteis, programme director at the University of Saskatchewan's Teaching and Learning Centre, has 18 years of teaching experience and 12 years concurrently in faculty development. She presents and writes extensively on a broad array of topics related to the scholarship of teaching and learning, and she is the author of her university's acclaimed teaching portfolio web site: http://www.usask.ca/tlc/teaching_portfolios/index.html.

Dennis M. Holt is a professor in the Division of Curriculum and Instruction at the University of North Florida. His contributions have included publications in the areas of arts education, computer education, teacher testing, music teacher education, and the professional development of teachers through regular and electronic portfolios.

Jeanette Hung holds an M.Ed. in counseling and is coordinator of career counseling services at Dalhousie University. Her expertise focuses on the complexities of career choice and development, and her interests include career decision making, portfolio development, career exploration and information, mid-career changes (reentry and job loss), fear, risk management, self-esteem, and communication skills.

Randall L. Kolar is associate professor of civil engineering at the University of Oklahoma, where his research interests center on computational hydraulics. He is principal investigator of the National Science Foundation–funded "Sooner City" project that seeks to integrate a common design project (civil infrastructure) across the curriculum and also promotes nontraditional classroom activities.

Paula McAllister earned her B.S. from Western Michigan University and her M.Ed. from University of North Florida. She is technology trainer for the Electronic Portfolio Partnership Project with the University of North Florida, Duval County public schools, and IBM Corporation.

Ted Panitz has been teaching for over 30 years, the last 26 at Cape Cod Community College. He has written extensively about writing across the curriculum and student-centered learning. Much of his work may be accessed at http://home.capecod.net/~tpanitz.

Zaide Pixley has been leading the First-Year Experience Program since 1996 at Kalamazoo College, one of 13 institutions of excellence in the first year chosen by the National Policy Center for the First Year of College. As assistant provost, Dr. Pixley oversees and teaches in the first-year seminar initiative, works closely with faculty on teaching and advising, and directs the college's electronic portfolio, peer leader, and first-year forum programs.

David A. Sabitini, professor and Sun Oil Company chair, joined the School of Civil Engineering and Environmental Science at the University of Oklahoma in 1989. His research has developed advanced technologies for subsurface remediation, environmentally friendly alternatives to organic solvents, and innovative techniques for improving engineering education.

Farland Stanley is the O'Brien Presidential Professor of Classics at the University of Oklahoma and director and founder of the university's Center for Classical Archaeology and Civilizations. His principal projects have been in Israel, Italy, Spain, and Portugal.

David A. Thomas teaches in the Bachelor of Interdisciplinary Studies Program at Arizona State University. Also a management consultant and business executive, he holds a Ph.D. in educational psychology and an M.B.A., with primary emphasis on human performance, adult learning and motivation, interdisciplinary team leadership, and teaching expertise.

Catherine M. Wehlburg is director of the Center for Teaching Excellence at Texas Christian University. Prior to this position, she was director of assessment and an associate professor in psychology at Stephens College.

H. David "Giz" Womack has a B.A. in both English and studio art and an M.B.A. from Wake Forest University, where he is information technology specialist in the Z. Smith Reynolds Library.

Contents

Foreword

Not long ago, an academic friend came into my office. He asked me how he could *really* tell what students had learned in his class. Examination scores, he said, were an obvious way to measure student learning: The higher the grade, the greater the learning. I told my friend that it was an obvious way, but that it struck me as more likely that examination scores or course grades were a measure of what students have retained, not necessarily what they have learned. True, a low test score might reflect inadequate learning, but it might also be no more than a reflection of the student's inability to articulate the full level of learning. Or, the particular test might not be the best vehicle for the student to demonstrate learning.

My friend pondered what I had told him. Okay, he said, if examination scores or course grades are flawed approaches to measuring deep student learning, is there a better way? I said that there is. It is the learning portfolio. My friend was not familiar with the concept and asked how he could learn more about it. *The Learning Portfolio: Reflective Practice for Improving Student Learning,* I told him, is the book you need. It covers just about everything you should know about print and electronic portfolios, gives models of successful use, and then provides sample learning portfolios and practical materials. Read it through, I advised; use it to understand what the learning portfolio is, how it can be used, what might go into it, and then decide how you can build it into your teaching. If you do that, you'll be able to tell better what students have *really* learned in your class.

The learning portfolio concept has gone well beyond the point of theoretical possibility. It has been used for more than 15 years. Today it is being adopted or pilot tested in various forms—paper-based or multimedia/online—by faculty in different disciplines in a rapidly increasing number of colleges and universities.

To create portfolios, students do three things. First, they collect their work, including notes for presentations, drafts of assignments, journals, homework, lab reports, class projects, critical essays, course listserv entries, research papers, and creative displays/performance. Then they select from this archive exhibits that demonstrate stipulated criteria such as best work, critical thinking, successive drafts, affective learning, practical application, and leadership. Finally, students reflect on their work by considering important guiding questions such as what they learned, why their learning is important, how they can apply key concepts in local and global contexts, how their learning has developed over the course of the term, and how they have used reflection to improve their performance.

All of this underscores a key point: In learning portfolios, students assume responsibility for documenting and interpreting their own learning. Through reflection, students make their thinking visible.

Since I use student learning portfolios in my own teaching, I asked the students in my organizational behavior class what they saw as the benefits of portfolios. Interestingly, their answers parallel those found in the literature. The students suggested the following benefits:

- They capture intellectual substance and deep learning in ways that other methods of evaluation cannot.

- They support the development, demonstration, and valid assessment of a wide range of personal, professional, and academic capabilities.

- They encourage students to take on important new roles in the documentation, observation, and review of their learning.

- They encourage improved student performance.

- They support the integration of learning from different parts of a course or program of study.

- They place some responsibility for assessing learning in the hands of the students instead of relying only on the judgment of others.

- They engage students in what they are learning so that transformation and internalization can take place.

- They lead students to relate new concepts to existing experience and critically evaluate and determine key themes.

- They show deep analysis of evidence and learning that stems from deep reflection.

A word about the importance of deep reflection. As college and university professors, we encourage our students to be reflective and to adopt reflective practices. But too often, such practices are passive and do not get beyond a "navel-gazing" activity. Perhaps the most commonly accepted means of recording student reflective practice is to retain a learning log. But merely recording what a student has learned is not sufficient. It does not indicate that deep reflection has taken place.

As John Zubizarreta points out in *The Learning Portfolio*, deep reflection—not a learning log—is at the very heart of the learning portfolio. It is the deliberate and systematic attention to a student's self-reflective, metacognitive appraisal of why and—importantly—how learning has occurred. Deep reflection allows students to focus on learning in a new way: It makes sense of the artifacts in a learning portfolio by converting the tacit knowledge in the evidence into explicit knowledge related to the student and his or her learning. The evidence is drawn together into a coherent tale of learning, of sense made, of new ideas developed, tested, and sometimes discarded. Through deep reflection, students explain what the evidence shows about what they have learned. They tell their own stories, assess their own strengths and weaknesses as learners, evaluate their products and performances, reflect on past learning, and think about paths for future learning.

How do students react to engaging in deep reflection as part of their learning portfolios? Consider these comment from students in my organizational behavior class:

> I confess that I was very skeptical at first. But when I reviewed the things that I put in my portfolio since the beginning of the semester, it became clear to me that some things were good and other things were not. I could really see how my understanding had developed during the course.

> My hypertext presentation made it easy to make references back and forth between reflection and evidence. The reflective part made the evidence come alive.

> I believe that all students can improve their learning by preparing a learning portfolio, especially if they include a significant reflective section.

Though my students today are quite supportive of learning portfolios, my understanding of learning portfolios has come late in my teaching career. And much of that understanding has come through trial and error. Because there was no reliable guide available, I had to experiment and struggle to find answers to questions such as: What does the term "portfolio" mean in a course? What kinds of student work should be included? How closely should the instructor specify the form, structure, size, and content of a learning portfolio? How much time does it take to put one together? What is the role of reflection? How does a mentor help?

Had *The Learning Portfolio* been available earlier, it would have answered virtually all of my questions. Clearly, this book has much to offer college professors who want to know more about portfolios. A particular strength is that it reviews generic issues in student learning portfolios that will be common to most practitioners, and it explores practices in a range of institutions.

The book draws together the accumulated knowledge and wisdom of John Zubizarreta and a host of worthy contributors from a wide range of institutions in the United States and Canada. The book offers an array of specific models of portfolio use across disciplines, courses, and programs, and the models can easily be adapted to different campuses. The broad scope of institutions represented includes, among others, Albion College, Arizona State University, Cape Cod Community College, Dalhousie University, Kalamazoo College, Kent State University, Longwood College, Radford University, and Wake Forest University.

The book also includes sample learning portfolios and practical materials. Because each portfolio is an individual document, varying importance has been assigned by different students to different items. Some students discuss an item at length while others dismiss it with just a sentence or two, or even omit it. That is as it should be. Although there is a general template for learning portfolios, much of what goes into them is determined by specific factors such as academic discipline, level of course or program, and personal preferences of the individual students who prepare them.

This book is unusually good. Clear, comprehensive, and immediately useful, it should be read by every faculty member who wants to know what students have *really* learned.

Peter Seldin
Distinguished Professor of Management
Pace University

Preface

The Learning Portfolio: Reflective Practice for Improving Student Learning is an effort to lodge the concept of learning portfolio development more firmly and higher on the agenda of higher education. The learning portfolio is a rich, convincing, and adaptable method of recording intellectual growth and involving students in a critically reflective, collaborative process that augments learning as a community endeavor and refines their educational experience. This book, then, is organized into four sections to offer readers both an academic understanding of and rationale for learning portfolios and practical information that can be custom tailored to suit many disciplinary, pedagogical, programmatic, and institutional needs.

OVERVIEW OF THE CONTENTS

Part I: About Student Learning Portfolios offers a foundation for and review of the value of reflective practice in student learning and how learning portfolios support reflection, sound assessment, and collaboration. I include a noticeably brief section on electronic portfolios, choosing not to dedicate too much time to the particular medium used in the production of portfolios. Instead, most of my attention is devoted to the principles, practice, and powerful rationale for portfolios and the common theoretical and practical learning issues that underlie portfolio development whether the product is paper or digital. The American Association for Higher Education, many college faculty development center and education department web sites, and a proliferating number of educational technology consultants have posted Internet sites and published monographs and handbooks about electronic portfolios, and the topic is well covered elsewhere. A staggering amount of information on electronic portfolios is increasingly available on the web, and the most helpful contribution I believe this book can make is to reaffirm the electronic portfolio's grounding in fundamental principles of learning portfolio development and point the reader to some of the numerous, useful Internet sites with expanding, complex links.

Chapter 1, An Overview of Student Learning Portfolios, offers a general background of the student portfolio movement and a rationale for implementing learning portfolios to improve and assess student learning, stressing the importance of reflection, documentation, and collaboration.

Chapter 2, Practical Questions and Issues About Student Learning Portfolios, defines the learning portfolio; addresses practical issues of time, length, and content; suggests a versatile, adaptable model; and emphasizes the importance of writing in portfolio development across disciplines and portfolio presentation choices.

Chapter 3, Important Factors in Developing and Using Student Learning Portfolios, elaborates the foundational value of reflective inquiry; collection, selection, and organization of evidence; and collaboration and mentoring in the process of developing and revising learning portfolios. The three crucial components of learning portfolios work together to promote improvement and sound, rigorous assessment of learning.

Chapter 4, Electronic Learning Portfolios, addresses the rapidly growing trend of electronic portfolios, discussing briefly the various ways in which multimedia and hypermedia technologies have transformed the development of learning portfolios in the digital age. The chapter also balances advantages and disadvantages, reminding us of the fundamentals inherent in print or electronic portfolios and shares a list of useful resources on electronic portfolios.

Part II: Models of Successful Use of Learning Portfolios includes diverse contributions by practitioners who implement portfolios in a variety of ways, including the use of digital technology. The array of specific models of how to use portfolios across disciplines, courses, and programs provides many practical ideas that can work on different campuses.

Part III: Sample Learning Portfolio Selections collects practical and adaptable examples of actual portfolios or parts of portfolios.

Part IV: Practical Materials collects a wealth of assignment sheets, guidelines, criteria, evaluation rubrics, and other materials used in developing print and electronic learning portfolios from across disciplines, programs, and types of institutions in higher education.

CONCLUSION

I have witnessed the remarkable growth and transformation of students as they engage in the process of developing their learning portfolios. They reflect in depth on their learning, their achievements, and their intellectual goals. They understand the satisfaction of taking ownership of their own learning. And they lay a foundation for their futures as lifelong learners. The learning portfolio is a rich learning tool. I hope that this book will help others to experience firsthand the rewards of the learning portfolio process.

John Zubizarreta

Acknowledgments

No book that makes a strong point about the importance of collaboration and mentoring in the learning enterprise would be complete without the author's recognition of the deep influence of a mentor in shaping the ideas and development of the volume. I owe Peter Seldin that debt. Peter has been a steady collaborator, inviting me to learn progressively with him more about portfolios to improve teaching, learning, and administration; his steady, generous mentoring has convinced me of the incalculable value of reflection, shared learning, and rigorous analysis of our work in the portfolio process. This book bears his stamp from cover to cover.

My other collaborators deserve my gratitude, too, for their diverse contributions have helped demonstrate the power of portfolios in enhancing student learning in various ways for different purposes. Some of the contributors spent extra energy in helping me find practical models of actual portfolios and teaching materials, making the volume useful and accessible across higher education. I am lucky to have worked with all of them on our project.

Most significantly, I want to thank my wife, Margie, and my two girls, Anna Ruth and Maria, for their patience, encouragement, and love. They have forgiven my many hours away from home at the office and my travels to conferences and consulting ventures out of town to build my portfolio knowledge and experience. I live and teach and learn for them.

PART I

About Student Learning Portfolios

Part I offers a foundation for and review of the value of reflective practice in student learning and how learning portfolios support reflection, sound assessment, and collaboration. It presents information about developing portfolios and answers to common concerns.

1) An Overview of Student Learning Portfolios

2) Practical Questions and Issues About Student Learning Portfolios

3) Important Factors in Developing and Using Student Learning Portfolios

4) Electronic Learning Portfolios

1

An Overview of Student Learning Portfolios

INTRODUCTION

The concept of the student portfolio has been widely known and implemented for some time in academic fields such as writing, communications, and the fine arts. Another popular application has been to provide a device for demonstrating the value of experiential learning or assessing credit for prior learning. Also, in business and teacher education, portfolios have been used commonly as effective tools for career preparation. Some portfolios are shared by students and faculty advisors for the purpose of academic and career advising. But such applications predominately have targeted the portfolio's efficacy in gathering judiciously selected products of student work in order to display content mastery or job readiness. Writing portfolios, for example, have been used generously in composition, creative writing, and other types of communication courses to present a diverse profile of a student's creative and technical skills. This type of portfolio is a rich addition to a teacher's comprehensive assessment of a student's growth during a particular course or at the end of a curricular program such as an academic major or a general education core with goals, objectives, and competencies in writing and other areas of oral or technological communication.

Similarly, portfolios have been a staple form of documentation of performance skills in the fine arts, providing both students and their teachers in the arts disciplines with a method for displaying and judging evidence of best practice and samples of the full range of talent. In other areas such as business, leadership, or teacher education, portfolios have been useful in supplying a mechanism for demonstrating a representative breadth of acquired skills for professional success. Burch (1997) suggests a few other uses of portfolios:

They can reveal, in the aggregate, the state of an academic
program; they can provide valuable insights into what students know and how they construct that knowledge; they
can provide institutional barometers, if you will, that suggest programmatic highs and lows, strengths and weaknesses. (p. 263)

A Focus on Learning

Often, however, what is left out of the formula in student portfolios is an
intentional focus on the learning piece, the deliberate and systematic attention not only to skills development but also to a student's self-reflective,
metacognitive appraisal of how and, more importantly, why learning has
occurred. This is not to assert, of course, that learning does not happen at
all when portfolios are used only as collection and organizing devices, that a
student does not benefit simply from the thoughtful act of choosing representative samples of accomplished work and making sense of the materials
as a display. But more enriched learning is likely to occur if the student is
encouraged to come to terms self-consciously over the duration of an academic endeavor—for example, a semester course, the culmination of an
honors program, the achievement of general education goals, or the completion of a degree—with essential questions about learning itself (see,
respectively, in this volume, Burges, Kolar and Sabitini; Bocchicchio, E.
Brown, Chambers; Wehlburg; or Brown and Womack):

- How have such products as those collected in a portfolio over time contributed to higher-order learning?

- What has the student learned from the process of generating the work?

- How does the work fit into a larger framework of lifelong learning
  which goes beyond simply completing graded assignments?

- Why was the work valuable in the student's overall cognitive development?

Such directed probing of the sources, coherence, and worth of learning—especially when combined with the power of collaboration and mentoring in making learning a recorded, shared, community endeavor—is
sometimes missing from the model of the student portfolio as simply an
individual repository of selected artifacts. To the point, analogously, the
same vital components frequently are lacking in what many faculty describe

as their teaching portfolios, prodigious folders that often are not much more than elaborate personnel files submitted confidentially at critical junctures in a professor's professional career.

Student portfolios, too, largely have been used to collect and evaluate students' work at key points in their progress, usually at the end of an academic endeavor; in a sense, the portfolio has been used primarily as a capstone product, sometimes even unintentionally minimizing the crucial learning process along the way in favor of the finished document, especially when the shine of fancy covers and graphics or glitz of digital enhancement become the student's focus, luring the teacher into similar pitfalls. Today, although exciting, positive innovations in electronic portfolios are increasingly emphasizing the importance of reflection (see, in this volume, Brown and Womack, Burges, Dunham, Holt and McAllister, and Pixley), the allure and dazzle of electronic media make the temptation toward product rather than process even greater.

Nevertheless, in truth, it would be difficult today to find a portfolio system that does not incorporate some element of critical reflection, even if the reflection amounts to the most rudimentary and form-generated statements about individual exhibits collected in a portfolio developed exclusively as a performance assessment or as a "vitae on steroids," as an acerbic voice once quipped about portfolio-based evaluation. One need not be so deprecatingly witty, however, because simply collecting artifacts for presentation and review purposes has the intrinsic worth of at least helping students to organize the outcomes of their efforts in a way that communicates accumulated skills and learning. Add a reflective component and learning portfolios, like teaching portfolios (Seldin, 1993, 1997), become "part of a process of monitoring ongoing professional growth, [encouraging] greater self-understanding [and becoming] effective tools for goal setting and self-directed learning" (Campbell, Melenyzer, Nettles, & Wyman, 2000, p. 14). In short, they become "part of a learning process" (Campbell, Melenyzer, Nettles, & Wyman, 2000, p. 14).

The authors just cited—writing about portfolios with a focus on product, largely from the utilitarian angle of how such documents serve as employment or credentialing tools for certification in teacher education—also make the strong point that in a well-managed portfolio project students should realize that their effort is not simply to construct "a scrapbook of college course assignments and memorabilia" (p. 2). Instead, even in a presentation portfolio (which the authors distinguish from a working portfolio), the product is also a process and should be construed as an "organized documentation of growth and achievement that provides tangible evidence of the attainment of professional knowledge, skills, and dispositions. Each portfolio is goal-driven, original, and reflective" (p. 13).

Survey Responses

Citing responses from a survey administered to students in a teacher certification program, Campbell, Melenyzer, Nettles, and Wyman (2000) demonstrate how students evidently "became aware of the full range of benefits of portfolio work" (p. 14):

> *Question: How have you benefited from the process of portfolio development?*

- "It has helped me to build confidence in myself as an educator."

- "Portfolio development has helped me to identify my strengths and weaknesses..."

- "I have become more aware of what future employers may be looking for..."

- "It is nice to be able to look back at everything I have accomplished throughout my college career."

- "The portfolio has helped me become more organized. It has helped me set goals and achieve them. I have a basis for my future education."

- "By having specific outcomes to accomplish, I am able to see exactly what areas of preparation I need to work on..."

- "The development of the portfolio has helped me see the importance of my work."

- "It made me strive to do my best work possible."

- "It helped me see the value of the assignments that I have completed in my classes. I take away more meaning from my work."

- "It has shown me how what I have learned all fits together."

- "The portfolio development itself is a means of becoming professional..."

- "I feel a sense of accomplishment . . . Being able to see your own growth and achievement is very exciting." (p. 15)

Undoubtedly, much more has happened to such students than the satisfaction of physically completing the task of collecting and organizing information, though their comments suggest appreciation for the portfolio's agency in preparing them for standards assessment and future careers. The testimonies also reveal a deeper sense of the value of reflective inquiry, the intrinsic merit of involving students in the power of reflection, the critically challenging act of thinking about their learning and making sense of the learning experience as a coherent, unified developmental process. Such thinking is the linchpin of lifelong, active learning, the key to helping students discover and understand what, how, and why they learn.

The portfolio approach to gauging student accomplishments and growth in learning—while not entirely new in higher education—has received more attention in the K–12 arena, as many of the sources consulted and cited in this book demonstrate. In English and a few other disciplines in college classes, portfolios and journals have been employed with some regularity, but remarkably, higher education has lagged behind the grade schools in innovating and refining such powerful learning tools. Today, following the groundswell of interest in teaching, course, and institutional portfolios, learning portfolios are beginning to attract significant attention in college and university settings. Arter and Spandel (1992); Gordon (1994); Wright, Knight, and Pomerleau (1999); and Cambridge (2001) are a few print resources. Barrett's (http://www.electronicportfolios.com) and the American Association for Higher Education's (http://aahe.ital.utexas.edu/electronic portfolios/index.html) web sites are among the numerous sources for online information on electronic portfolios. Following Seldin's (1993, 1997) work on teaching portfolios, learning portfolios are now rapidly becoming mainstream in higher education.

THE IMPORTANCE OF REFLECTIVE INQUIRY

The crucial element of reflection is the key to marshaling the power of what I call learning portfolios, and I will return to the theme in Chapter 3. I dwell on reflection precisely because of my emphasis on how reflective thinking and judgment are effective stimuli to deep, lasting learning. Certainly, such reflection is desirable in promoting better learning, but it is also challenging and painful, demanding a level of self-scrutiny, honesty, and disinterestedness which comes with great difficulty. As John Dewey (1910) proclaims:

> Reflective thinking is always more or less troublesome because it involves overcoming the inertia that inclines one to accept suggestions at their face value; it involves willingness to endure a condition of mental unrest and disturbance. Reflective thinking, in short, means judgment suspended during further inquiry; and suspense is likely to be somewhat painful. . . . To maintain the state of doubt and to carry on systematic and protracted inquiry—these are the essentials of thinking. (p. 13)

Questions for Reflection in Portfolios

This book argues that the durable value of portfolios in improving student learning resides in engaging students not just in collecting representative samples of their work for assessment, evaluation, or career preparation but in addressing vital reflective questions that invite systematic and protracted inquiry:

- What have I learned? Why did I learn?
- When have I learned? In what circumstances? Under what conditions?
- How have I learned or not, and do I know what kind of learner I am?
- How does what I have learned fit into a full, continual plan for learning?
- What difference has the learning made in my intellectual, personal, and ethical development?
- In what ways is what I have learned valuable to have learned at all?

Obviously, many more questions come to mind as one begins to fashion a strategy for reflection. Fink (2001), sharing a keen interest in learning portfolios, suggests:

> [S]tudents may comment on the way they were challenged to analyze new ideas; or they may report on the excitement generated by mastering complex material; or they may describe how they came away from the class with a new, more positive attitude for the subject matter. In addition, the development of the learning portfolio may ask the students to address such personal issues as: "Was this class

enjoyable, exciting, interesting?" or "How did this class relate to your personal beliefs and/or prior knowledge about the subject matter?" (p. 1)

Linking his innovative taxonomy of higher-level learning to his understanding of how learning portfolios facilitate metacognitive processes that lead to greater leaps in knowing how and why one has changed as a result of learning, Fink (2001) also provides an example of how carefully formulated questions can yield fruitful reflective learning in the case of students' internships:

> I recently had occasion to interview a pair of students who had participated in a summer internship in Washington, DC, and who were trying to prepare future interns. During the interview, I posed a series of questions focused on each of the components.
>
> 1) During the time you were working as an intern, how did you change, in terms of
>
>   • What you care about differently now, than you did before?
>
>   • What actions you are capable of performing now?
>
>   • What you can connect or integrate now, that you could not before?
>
>   • Your ability to think about problems in political science?
>
>   • What you know?
>
> 2) What did you learn about
>
>   • The process of learning about politics?
>
>   • Interacting with other people?
>
>   • Yourself?
>
>   • Some of the major ideas you studied in political science?
>
>   • The phenomena involved (in this case, politics)?
>
> The answers from the two students were different from each other, very focused, and very rich. (pp. 127–128)

In the context of a methods course, Yancey (1997) reports having student teachers respond to questions in portfolios structured to promote students' reflections on their learning progress as prospective novice instructors:

- "What have you learned so far in this class?"

- "Is this what you expected to learn?"

- "What else do you need to learn?"

- "How will you go about learning it?" (p. 252)

Guiding students toward the metacognitive work necessary for higher-level composition and strong critical thinking skills, Claywell (2001) begins nearly every section of her book on portfolios with directed questions for reflection on purpose, content, format, process, and evaluation of learning. Here are some examples, slightly modified to make them practical across a variety of disciplines:

- How will your portfolio be used? Who is the audience for your portfolio? What is the role of that audience? (p. 1)

- What have you learned about the subject that you did not previously know? What have you discovered about your learning style? (p. 20)

- What are the best examples of your work for this project? The worst? Why? (p. 33)

- What do the pieces and the portfolio reflect overall about your learning? (p. 35)

- What new learning strategies have you adopted as a result of the portfolio process? (p. 43)

- What were the most difficult parts of the process? Why? (p. 49)

- In what ways do your reflections reveal what makes your portfolio unique? What specific features of the class were beneficial in your learning? Your personal voice? How do your reflections point to specific changes in the actual revisions in the portfolio? The improved knowledge you have gained? The growth you have made as a scholar? (p. 52)

• What has been meaningful about the portfolio process? (p. 65)

What is particularly instructive and liberating about the questions suggested by Fink, Yancey, Claywell, and others who employ portfolio strategies in improving and assessing student learning is that the queries motivate students to professionalize their responses to the enterprise of education by taking seriously the underlying pedagogical as well as overt methodological reasons for learning. Attaining this professional, disinterested attitude toward learning is an important lesson in mature, critical thinking for all students. In a sense, students are empowered to know and make sense of the sources and outcomes of their learning, acquiring not just the skills necessary for effective learning and goal setting but essentially a habit of being, an approach to knowing and learning—indeed, to life itself—grounded in critical reflection.

LEARNING AS COMMUNITY

Such reflection is facilitated best not by leaving students individually to their own devices in thinking about their learning but by utilizing the advantages of collaboration and mentoring in making learning community property. The idea here is not to suggest tactics that would violate personal and legal boundaries of privacy but rather to endorse the premise that learning is enhanced by recognizing its relational values, by helping students connect individual pieces of gained knowledge to a larger puzzle of learning with ever-widening intellectual, material, ethical, social, and even spiritual implications. Deep, lasting learning is also relational in the sense that what students learn in the classroom ideally must relate sensibly to their felt lives, must provide avenues for them to connect the abstractions of academic pursuits to the realities of immediate experience. Dewey (1910), once again, provides us with the needed insight:

> Instruction always runs the risk of swamping the pupil's own vital, though narrow, experience under masses of communicated material. The instructor ceases and the teacher begins at the point where communicated matter stimulates into fuller and more significant life that which has entered by the strait and narrow gate of sense perception and motor activity. Genuine communication involves contagion; its name should not be taken in vain by terming communication that which produces no community of thought and

> purpose between the [student] and the race of which he is
> the heir. (p. 224)

In other words, dissemination of facts and delivery of knowledge are acts of instruction which serve an important but hierarchically lower purpose in how we think and learn. Higher-order teaching and learning are the shared acts of a reflective discourse community, a dynamic collaborative of living ideas that transform both teacher and learner.

The relationship with an influential mentor adds the collaborative edge that makes the human difference in moving students (and teachers) along a continuum of learning. Collaborators and mentors—whether peers or teachers (either or both can be helpful catalysts in the process of developing portfolios)—are vital agents in moving students in the right direction toward more meaningful learning, toward knowledge and insights that they can relate to other academic discoveries and to other dimensions of their personal experiences. Recent developments in the available scholarship on student portfolios suggest that more educators are recognizing the acute importance of such reflection in portfolios, and happily a trend toward emphasizing the reflective, process-oriented component of student portfolios (as opposed to its twin function of collecting selected samples of representative work for assessment) is emerging. I would add to the trend that reflection, an inherently private act, is sharpened by the positive influence of collaboration with a mentor in developing and reviewing a learning portfolio.

Campbell, Melenyzer, Nettles, and Wyman (2000) agree that collaboration is important. Commenting that

> students left alone to do portfolio work . . . tend to focus
> on organizing and justifying documentation of what they
> have already done well, [the authors argue that] it takes
> encounters with peers, faculty facilitators, and members of
> the larger professional community to challenge progress
> toward growing and changing, setting new goals, and
> designing new strategies for professional development. . . .
> the more collaborative portfolio work becomes, the greater
> the growth in meeting the standards [of higher-level learn-
> ing]. (pp. *ix–x*)

THE ARGUMENT FOR LEARNING PORTFOLIOS

This book sheds further light on how and why the portfolio contributes to students' sophisticated learning by exploring how strategies of reflective practice, especially when conjoined with the supportive influence of mentoring, can be applied to improve and document student learning. Engaging students not only in collecting selected samples of their work for assessment, evaluation, and career development but also in continuous, collaborative reflection about the process of learning is a powerful complement to traditional measures of student achievement. In her book on learning journals, kin to the format and function of learning portfolios, Moon (1999) summarizes the various ways in which students benefit from reflective activity and organized assessment. She argues that journals (or portfolios, in my rephrasing) create "conditions that favour learning":

- Portfolios demand time and intellectual space.

- The independent and self-directing nature of the process develops a sense of ownership of the learning in the learner.

- Portfolios focus attention on particular areas of, and demand the independent ordering of, thought.

- Portfolios often draw affective function into learning and this can bring about greater effectiveness in learning.

- The ill-structured nature of the tasks involved in portfolio development challenges a learner and increases the sophistication of the learning process. (p. 34)

Moon also suggests that creating frameworks such as learning portfolios for students to reflect progressively on their work provides

> an opportunity for a range of forms of learning activities, [such as] learning about self (self-development); learning to resolve uncertainty or to reach decisions; learning that brings about empowerment or emancipation. Sometimes the learning that arises from reflection may be unexpected. (p. 34)

Finally, she adds that learning journals or portfolios stimulate and support learning across diverse disciplines by encouraging "reflective thinking and writing, which are associated with deeper forms of learning and better learning outcomes, [and by fostering the] metacognition . . . associated with expertise in learning" (p. 35).

Alan Wright, one of the chief players behind Canada's Dalhousie University's formidable Career Portfolio Program (see Hung, in this volume), offers apt testimony to the value of such reflective writing even when it is not ostensibly the main purpose of a student's portfolio: "Although the employment parlance is what gets us the grants to do our work at Dal, the practice shows that the reflective component is crucial to the success of the enterprise" (July 26, 2001, personal communication). Again, the crossover lessons of the teaching portfolio's premium on the "special power" of reflection apply to the learning portfolio (Seldin, 1993, p. 9).

In the next chapter, I will address some of the practical considerations involved in using student learning portfolios, such as time involved, length, and content.

2

Practical Questions and Issues About Student Learning Portfolios

WHAT IS A LEARNING PORTFOLIO?

The numerous contributions in Part II of this volume attest to the multiple approaches to engaging students in portfolio development. I would venture, however, a model that broadly approximates in the field of student learning what the teaching portfolio offers in the field of teaching performance. In the work of Edgerton, Hutchings, and Quinlan (1991); Hutchings (1998); Murray (1995); Seldin (1993, 1997); Shore, et al. (1986); Zubizarreta (1994, 1995, 1997); and other advocates of portfolio strategies, the premium value of teaching portfolios is improvement through the continual process of reflection tied to mentoring, rigorous assessment, and documentation. Likewise, the primary motive of the learning portfolio is to improve student learning by providing a structure for students to reflect systematically over time on the learning process and to develop the aptitudes, skills, and habits that come from critical reflection. Following paradigms of learning such as those found in Brookfield's (1995), Dewey's (1910), Kolb's (1984), or Schön's (1983, 1987) theories of reflection; Bloom's (1956) taxonomy of educational objectives; or Fink's (2001, 2003) experimental model of "higher-level learning," such thinking about the process of learning forms the heart of the learning portfolio.

Sharing my values, Annis and Jones (1995) offer a brief definition of student portfolios: "A portfolio can be defined as a multidimensional, documented collection of . . . a . . . student's work put together in an organized way and including a reflective discussion of the materials contained in the portfolio" (pp. 181–182). I suggest the following definition that allows for proper flexibility across disciplinary purposes and designs:

The learning portfolio is a flexible, evidence-based tool that engages students in a process of continuous reflection and collaborative analysis of learning. As written text, electronic display, or other creative project, the portfolio captures the scope, richness, and relevance of students' learning. The portfolio focuses on purposefully and collaboratively selected reflections and evidence for both improvement and assessment of students' learning.

TIME COMMITMENT

Let's cut to the chase. Recognizing that both students and faculty justifiably will resist any methodology or instrument that is nothing more than an add-on to course activities and requirements, I issue a strong word of caution at the outset before pondering a model. As a teacher myself, I know time is a paramount issue. Learning portfolios must be an idea driven by philosophical and pedagogical goals integrated into a course in such a way to contribute qualitatively, not necessarily quantitatively, to the learning/teaching enterprise. Moon (1999) reinforces the message: "Time is an issue," for while learning portfolios create a positive "intellectual space for learners," the considerable time involved "is a major reason for the abandonment" of such projects (p. 79).

LENGTH

Sensitive to the issue of time, I envision a model that is not an unwieldy repository of continually expanding artifacts and reflective commentaries, the variety of student portfolio in which students are asked to collect scores of exhibits and write prescribed narratives, prompted by a standardized list of questions for each item. Instead, my sense is that less is better, especially if the portfolio author enlists the aid of a collaborative mentor who helps provide feedback in making decisions about purpose, content, format, and selectivity of appendix materials. The mentor might be an assigned or self-selected peer in a course, a veteran peer in a major or program, a teacher, an academic advisor, or a program director. The mentor is not so much an expert or evaluator as a collaborator who assists the author in identifying the rationale for selectivity of information and in carrying out a thoughtful plan for developing a succinct but sound portfolio that meets the needs of the learner. One major responsibility of the mentor is to keep the portfolio manageable in size by pressing for a concise, reflective narrative plus judiciously selected evidence in a series of appropriate appendices.

The parameter of a few narrative pages, plus appendices, is obviously a flexible benchmark. In any case, the portfolio never outgrows its practical boundaries for the sake of both author and designated audience, if any. In the instance of a portfolio created as a profile of learning over a long period of time, I recommend that as new materials are added, old ones are removed, keeping the act of revision active and refreshing, continually informing the learning process. Conceivably, an anthology of progressive drafts or a bank of smaller course portfolios could be assembled to form a substantive, revealing history of learning.

CONTENT

What are the contents of a learning portfolio? There is no right or complete answer. Portfolios vary in purpose, and different purposes determine the diverse contents. Generally, the learning portfolio I have in mind consists of a carefully reasoned, reflective narrative that, depending on purpose, captures the scope, progress, and value of learning, complemented by an equally representative compilation of concrete evidence. A popular alternative is a number of short reflections on separate or grouped items of evidence, though I prefer the coherence and unity of reflective analysis required in a single reflective statement and overview with keyed references to evidence in an appendix.

In Chapter 3, I discuss further the issue of evidence, providing representative examples of items that may be included in a portfolio, but here is a very generic table of contents, organized by broad categories and certainly not prescriptive or exhaustive. The table is meant to be suggestive, inviting multidisciplinary ideas of what the actual, complex contents of a student portfolio might be, remembering the caveat that purpose will drive final decisions about both reflection and documentation:

Table of Contents

1) *Philosophy of Learning* (reflective narrative on learning process)

2) *Achievements in Learning* (transcripts, course descriptions, résumés, honors, awards, internships, tutoring)

3) *Evidence of Learning* (research papers, critical essays, field experience logs, creative displays/performances, data/spreadsheet analyses, course listserv entries)

4) *Assessment of Learning* (instructor feedback, course test scores, exit/board exams, lab/data reviews, research project results, practicum reports)

5) *Relevance of Learning* (practical applications, leadership, relation of learning to personal and professional domains, ethical/moral growth, affiliations, hobbies, volunteering, affective value of learning)

6) *Learning Goals* (plans to enhance, connect, and apply learning)

7) *Appendices* (selected documentation)

The general categories of the table, again, are suggestive; each portfolio project will define specific contents in different ways, depending on purpose and learning objectives. But it is worth noting that the categories reflect a logical pattern, one that essentially mirrors sound practice for both improvement and assessment. The flow parallels this order of reflective analysis, complemented by documentation in the appendix:

- What, how, when, and why did I learn?

- What have I accomplished with my learning?

- What products and/or outcomes do I have to demonstrate learning?

- What measures and accounting do I have of my learning?

- What difference has learning made in my life?

- What plans do I have to continue learning?

- What supporting evidence do I have?

A brief reflective section of just a few pages, plus appendices, is a practical investment for the student, who benefits from the efficacy of portfolio development in bolstering learning. The teacher, too, gains a multifaceted means of appreciating, understanding, and assessing a student's learning. The portfolio may range from detailing specific gains made in a single course or designated part of a course to plotting a student's learning in an entire academic program (see, respectively, in this volume, Kolar and Sabitini, Panitz, and Wehlburg).

The increasing popularity of electronic student portfolios naturally encourages us to rethink the criterion of length or the issue of content because of the awesome capability of hypertext medium. The point is illustrated by a glance at some of the samples of digitized portfolios in this volume or at the proliferation of student portfolios on the web (see several references in the Selected Resources section of Chapter 4). Chapter 4 addresses some of the ways in which analog and digital technologies have contributed to new, exciting models of portfolio development, but even with the marvels of computerization, I emphasize the cautionary note of keeping the portfolio process manageable and coherent, focused on meaningful reflection and selective evidence rather than on many pages of writing or overwhelming hyperlinks and flashy technical display.

A MODEL FOR THE LEARNING PORTFOLIO

Recognizing that student portfolios take many forms, depending on purpose and design (as the diverse summaries and examples included later in this volume demonstrate), I propose a rather simple model for the learning portfolio which is predicated on three fundamental components found also in teaching portfolios (Seldin, 1993, 1997):

- Reflection

- Documentation

- Collaboration

The result is a compact, strategically organized document that evolves qualitatively to reflect the dynamic nature of engaged learning. Multiple revisions are encouraged as desirable spotlights on progress, each draft tightly structured and manageable, revealing over time a student's individual pattern of intellectual and personal growth. Drafts may be textual revisions, updated documentation, or redesigned web pages, depending on the type of portfolio and disciplinary preferences, but the process nature of ongoing reflection is fundamental to the improvement agency of learning portfolios. Instructors need not provide lengthy feedback on each draft, but the insights gained into a student's progress offers teachers opportunities for better assessment and more positive influence on learning through closer mentoring.

Not at all prescriptive, the model obviously synthesizes the basic, sound elements of the many versions of student portfolios represented later in Part II, and it may be adapted in myriad ways to suit individual needs. Flexibility, of course, is as key to learning as it is to portfolio development. Yancey (1997) underscores this point in her own reflections about her dynamic use of portfolios with teacher protégés in a methods class:

> [If we think of it] as a professional text, we . . . lose the
> chance to learn from the portfolio what it can teach us:

that the only way that it can teach us is by not being too
rigid, too fixed, too ... professional in its construction; that
allowing freedom in it provide[s] one way for students'
voices to be heard. ... (p. 259)

A learning portfolio that is flexible in design, goals, and outcomes, and
is easily adaptable to a variety of disciplines and purposes, is a strong model.
Figure 2.1 graphically conceptualizes a learning portfolio.

Figure 2.1

The Learning Portfolio

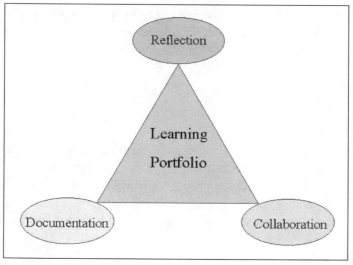

Notice that maximum learning occurs when reflection, documentation,
and collaboration come together in the center of the design. To be sure,
learning occurs even when only one of the domains is activated. For example, a student may gain valuable insight into the quality of a learning experience solely by the private act of thinking critically about one's progress; by
the basic, physical gathering and organization of available artifacts or evidence; or by reaping the benefits of collaboration and mentoring inherent
in accepting another's challenging insights and perspectives.

When any two of the components of the educational process are
tapped, the potential for better learning increases. Hence, the student who
joins reflection with evidence to think about how completed work reveals a
pattern of positive learning capitalizes on the best features of portfolio

designs that combine exhibits of learning with reflective statements about achievements and goals. The student who partners with a peer or faculty mentor to take advantage of directed discourse and feedback about one's own reflections benefits from the virtues of collaboration in building learning community.

Arguably, the student who pulls all three domains together stands a greater chance of transforming an incidental learning activity into a deeper, enduring learning process. By providing a structure that is essentially an act of communication—that is, an investment in learning as community—the learning portfolio concept, primarily through the powerful agency of reviewed work, facilitates students' active engagement of the three crucial domains: 1) reflections on learning, 2) evidence and outcomes of learning, and 3) collaboration and mentoring.

Moon (1999) offers a much more elaborate and visually complex model of the reflective learning process. Her concept map is a useful complement to the simplicity of the tripartite figure. Her design maps a course from initial reflection to resolution, but I would add another step, accounting for the influence of consultation with a mentor—a teacher, course peer, senior student, or academic advisor, for instance—a significant spark for reflective learning.

THE POWER OF WRITING AND LEARNING PORTFOLIOS

The engine that drives much of the success of the learning portfolio and many other strategies of collaborative and cooperative learning, active learning, classroom assessment techniques, problem-based learning, and reflective practice is the power of writing. Moon (1999), relying on key ideas from several sources in the vast literature on process rhetoric and composition, underscores the ways in which writing is a powerful method of learning:

- Writing forces learners to take time for reflection.

- Writing forces learners to organize and to clarify their thoughts in order to sequence them in a linear manner. In this way they reflect on and improve their understanding.

- Writing causes learners to focus their attention. It forces activity in the learner.

- Writing helps learners to know whether or not they understand something. If they cannot explain it, they probably cannot understand it.

- Along similar lines, being asked to write the explanation of something can encourage a deep approach to learning in the manner that the learner anticipates the quality of understanding required for the writing.

- Writing an account of something enables the writer to talk about it more clearly.

- Writing captures ideas for later consideration.

- Writing sets up a self-provided feedback system.

- Writing can record a train of thought and relate it in past, present, and future.

- The process of writing is creative and develops new structures. It can be enjoyable.

- The pace of writing slows the pace of thinking and can thereby increase its effectiveness. (p. 31)

As an engaged process of learning, the writing that anchors portfolio development—whether the portfolio is a text document, creative project, or web site with multiple hypertext links—stimulates in the learner not only the conventional aspects of invention, composition, and revision inherent in writing with a purpose but also the complex dimensions of selecting representative samples of one's work, thinking about how and why such information reveals higher-level learning, maintaining currency and vitality in the compilation of materials, and evaluating the relevance and significance of such work. Weiser (1997), focusing on portfolios designed to improve and assess students' writing abilities, adds:

> Portfolios allow us to consider the writing process in a broader context than the familiar planning, drafting, revising, editing concept of process does. While revision is an inherent part of portfolio approaches, the decision to use portfolios as the means of evaluating students' writing ability and development extends the process to include additional decision-making conditions: the *collection* of writing, *reflection* about that writing, the *selection* of pieces to

be further revised for the final evaluation, the *revision* of those pieces, and finally their *evaluation*. Each of these, often overlapping practices, contributes to both students' and teachers' extended understanding of what it means to write. (p. 296)

Many writing teachers have held tight to such ideas, including, representatively, Bean (1996), Emig (1971, 1977), Hayes and Flower (1980), Hillocks (1995), and Lindemann (1982). But the foundation established by the composition and rhetoric revolution of the last few decades is equally applicable to other disciplines. The variety of ways in which writing can be used as a tool for disciplinary learning has been at the front of writing across the curriculum programs, and some innovative approaches are described and shared in summaries and models included later in this volume. Such exciting developments in the use of writing for learning across disciplinary lines have been instrumental in triggering and valorizing the numerous pedagogies that rely on writing as a vehicle for reflection, as a structure for learning in a variety of disciplines.

3

Important Factors in Developing and Using Student Learning Portfolios

REFLECTION

The model I have proposed for the learning portfolio stresses the interplay among the three vital elements of reflection, evidence, and collaboration or mentoring. Sustaining the process of developing and revising the portfolio is the power of writing as a corollary to thinking and learning as well as a creative and facilitative activity for recording, assessing, improving, and evaluating learning. The learning portfolio, therefore, consists of a written narrative section in which the student reflects critically about essential questions of what, when, how, and why learning has occurred. In the course of such introspective analysis, the student is guided to think further about how specific acts of learning—for instance, a seminar or lab course, a special writing assignment in a class, a long-term undergraduate research project, a field experience or internship, an interdisciplinary core, or an honors program of study—have contributed to a coherent, developmental, interrelated process of learning.

I point out that in the extensive literature about teaching portfolios, critical reflection is cited repeatedly as the main stimulus to improvement of practice. While the portfolio is widely implemented as a "relevant, valid, useful component of a teaching evaluation system" (Zubizarreta, 1999, p. 164), the primary benefit of teaching portfolio development is improvement, a chief motivation for "engaging in the reflection and documentation that comprise a portfolio" (Seldin, Annis, & Zubizarreta, 1995, p. 60). Such enhancement of teaching performance occurs as a result of the mentoring and systematic self-analysis that characterize the process of reflection in writing a reliable and valid portfolio. Seldin (1997), the leading voice on teaching portfolios, captures the message of the power of reflection: "In truth, one of the most significant parts of the portfolio is the faculty member's self-reflection on his or her teaching. Preparing it can help professors unearth new discoveries about themselves as teachers" (p. 8).

Similarly, learning portfolios emphasize that students' knowledge and, more significantly, their understanding of how and why such knowledge fits into a larger framework of cognitive and emotional development are fundamentally connected to the opportunities they have to reflect critically on their education and on the very meaning of learning itself. Learning portfolios help students unearth new discoveries about themselves as learners.

But students do not automatically know how to reflect to advantage; they may lack the skills of reflection or they may confuse reflective inquiry with untempered emotional unloading. Brookfield's (1995) guidelines for his students' learning journals are excellent reminders of how important it is to approach the use of such learning tools carefully and to be deliberate and clear in expressing expectations to students. Perry (1997) also warns,

> Most importantly, the purpose and audience of any portfolio must be explicit. Moreover, the purpose must be meaningful to the students. All students do not have to assemble portfolios for the same purposes and audiences, but all must have explicit rubrics for scoring. (p. 188)

Examples of such rubrics are shared in Part III of this volume, and Campbell, Melenyzer, Nettles, and Wyman (2000) offer handy checkpoint lists. Additional evaluation models are found in Martin-Kniep's (1999) book on professional portfolios and at one of the many links in Barrett's (2000b) web site on electronic portfolios (http://transition.alaska.edu/www/port folios/EPDevProcess.html#eval). The clarity and useful guidance provided by such detailed expectations and evaluation criteria promote more focused, substantive reflection on the part of students. Without such planning and precision on the part of teachers, students will have a reduced chance of embracing the challenges and rewards of reflective practice.

Drawing from a portfolio project she helped implement among K–12 instructors, D'Aoust (1992) points out that although many teachers "considered reflection to be a critical component of using portfolios, they also discovered that it was the most difficult 'to teach.' The difficulty was that most students lacked a vocabulary enabling reflection" (p. 44). D'Aoust further reveals how the teachers "found that, in order to initiate and sustain student reflection, they needed to structure specific questions for the students" (p. 44). The following are some examples from D'Aoust's account, freely modified to suggest how such prompts can be used across disciplines for students' self-analysis of their development as learners:

- How am I doing on this lab report or paper assignment?

- Where am I headed in this statistical summary and analysis?

- How does this piece of writing compare with my other writing?

- How did I sustain my interest in collecting this data?

- Did collaborating with peers or with my instructor help me better achieve learning goals of my practicum?

- How would I describe my progress as a learner in my major, and what evidence can I give in my portfolio?

- Where do I need help as a learner in my chosen field?

- How can a peer mentor or the teacher assist me to become a better learner?

D'Aoust's samples are easily adapted to other disciplinary areas, and the underlying advantage of designing such probes in any context is that students begin to develop a vocabulary of reflection, a means for communicating to themselves, to each other, and to external evaluators the individual character and progress of their learning.

Brookfield's (1995) instructions and questions on keeping a learning journal are worth sharing at length, too:

> The purpose of this journal...will give you some insight into your own emotional and cognitive rhythms as a learner. By this, I mean that you will become more aware of how you go about organizing your learning, what kinds of learning tasks you are drawn to, what teaching styles you find most congenial, what tasks you resist and seek to avoid, what conditions encourage you to take risks in learning.... If you'd like some structure to help you with the first few weeks' entries, try writing a few lines in response to the following questions:
>
> - What have I learned this week about myself as a learner?

- What have I learned this week about my emotional responses to learning?

- What were the highest emotional moments in my learning activities this week?

- What were the lowest emotional moments in my learning activities this week?

- What learning tasks did I respond to most easily this week?

- What learning tasks gave me the greatest difficulties this week?

- What was the most significant thing that happened to me as a learner this week?

- What learning activity or emotional response most took me by surprise this week?

- Of everything I did this week in my learning, what would I do differently if I had to do it again?

- What do I feel proudest about regarding my learning activities this week?

- What do I feel most dissatisfied with regarding my learning activities this week?

(pp. 97–98)

Clearly, Brookfield is communicating to students that getting beyond the acquisition of presumably known facts to questioning received knowledge and then to self-examining the complex epistemological process involved in knowing ourselves and our world is the hallmark of critical thinking, higher-order learning, and reflective judgment. The learning portfolio, installed in any of its numerous print or electronic manifestations in a student's educational progress, provides a vehicle for such practiced reflection.

EVIDENCE AND OUTCOMES OF LEARNING

Complementing portions of reflective narrative, an appendix of documentary materials balances the portfolio by providing concrete evidence of the student's claims, descriptions, analyses, and reflections. The narrative must include methodical references throughout to documentary materials in the appendix, linking reflection and evidence in a sound representation of the extent, meaning, and value of a student's learning. If, in the course of the reflective narrative, a student suggests gained mastery of a specific skill or aspect of disciplinary content, then a keyed reference to evidence in a corresponding appendix will substantiate what the student has learned. In an electronic portfolio, the reference would be a hypertext link.

No matter the medium of expression, the benefit to the student is an opportunity to engage in self-examination of what has been learned in an assignment, a course, or a program; how it has been applied; why the learning has been valuable; and to what extent the product of learning meets educational standards and goals. The combination of reflection and documentation encourages the student to articulate the core aims of portfolio development:

- Engage students in a process of inquiry into what they have learned.

- Provide students with a model for demonstrating the outcomes of learning.

- Establish a reflective learning environment that helps students go beyond accumulation of knowledge to analysis of how, when, and why they have learned.

- Promote thinking about what lies ahead for improvement and future learning.

The process of such reflection tied to evidence promotes a sophisticated, mature learning experience that closes the assessment loop from assertion, to demonstration, to analysis, to evaluation, to goals. Such coherence between reflective narrative and materials in the appendix is necessary to stem the potential influence of what Weiser (1997) calls the "schmooze" and "glow" (pp. 300–301) of reflective writing which can skew—in either positive or negative ways—the authenticity of portfolio work.

The problems uncovered by Weiser's shrewd analysis are real and common enough to merit some attention here. A portfolio system—relying heavily on qualitative information and on a student's ability to communicate meaningful gains in learning—can easily lose sight of substance. One cause of resistance to implementation of student portfolios (the same is true of faculty teaching portfolios) is the complaint that portfolios too easily risk the shine of rhetoric, the potentially blinding effect of persuasive writing, solicitous tone, and perhaps invented achievement. Possibly, the portfolio may even fabricate the prized outcome of improvement based on falsely engineered products that seemingly detail progress from lesser to greater skills and accomplishments. I have mentored many faculty in developing teaching portfolios, and I have heard the same suspicions about faculty portfolios as ongoing displays of professional improvement. Faculty might ask, "Why articulate lofty, challenging goals when one can set sights lower and demonstrate progress by leaps and bounds?" Students might ask, "Why do my best on an essay assignment or lab project when I can ratchet down a first effort and then produce a much better final endeavor?"

Brookfield (1995) points out yet another fascinating possibility that may happen inadvertently when learning portfolios stress the importance of reflection and students misinterpret the message to mean that they must find ways to hype their self-reporting:

> Student journals, portfolios, and learning logs are all the rage among teachers who advocate experiential methods. Teachers believe that encouraging students to speak personally and directly about their experiences honors and encourages their authentic voices. That this often happens is undeniable. However, journals, portfolios, and logs also have the potential to become ritualistic and mandated confessionals... the educational equivalents of the tabloid-like, sensationalistic outpourings of talk show participants. (p. 13)

Such mixed messages are a tricky problem in setting up requirements for a learning portfolio project, and the teacher must be fully aware of students' difficulty in navigating between the risks of denial and distortion, as Brookfield puts it, and the transformative and liberating benefits of critical reflection. Add to such suspicions and predicaments the fear of how writing skills, glitzy covers and formats, or the digital enhancements of web pages, presentation software, or CD-ROM technology can color the fair, objective assessment of portfolios, and it is easy to see why some resistance occurs.

The obstacles mentioned here are addressed by the nonnegotiable requirement that learning portfolios must consist of more than the reflective narrative, even though reflection forms the core of the process. Reflective thought must be tied to real evidence, a lesson Brookfield (1995) takes on in a much broader, polemical context, arguing finally that "reflection in and of itself is not enough: it must always be linked to how the world can be changed" (p. 217). In his definition of critical reflection as it applies to improvement of teaching, Brookfield outlines four lenses available to the critically reflective practitioner for viewing and analyzing one's individual performance and hegemonic assumptions about the teaching enterprise:

1) Autobiographical reflection

2) Our students' eyes

3) Colleagues' perceptions and experiences

4) Theoretical literature

Without much force, we can apply virtually the same principles to the successful use of learning portfolios. Students, exactly like faculty, easily buy into the hegemony of improvement—that is, into the collectively accepted notion that what matters most in assessment and evaluation of learning and teaching is the extent to which we can demonstrate positive, ongoing progress and growth. While the principle is admirable and sound in many ways, both students and teachers must guard against the subtle lure to concentrate on reflecting about the outcome of change without critically examining the nature and worth of change itself. Learners must ask themselves key questions about the assumed value of improvement:

• Was change necessary?

• What process did I use to facilitate change?

• How has change affected the way I work?

• Why was the change desirable?

• What evidence do I have that I am a better learner because of change?

The skeptical posture of such reflection goes beyond simply meeting imperatives of improvement. Having critically questioned the very foundation of an assumption that undergirds even this volume—the assumption that reflective inquiry is at the heart of higher-level learning and portfolio development—the practiced reflective learner realizes that a creditable learning portfolio depends on purposefully selected, collaboratively reviewed, diverse documentation for complete efficacy. To borrow Brookfield's metaphor, we need multiple lenses through which to view and understand the phenomenon of learning, necessitating, among other things, clear, detailed, thoughtful documentation.

As I have suggested earlier in this chapter, the documentation in the appendix is the leveler needed to stem hesitations about the undue influence of form over content. Students clever enough to manufacture work of lesser quality to play against improved work later cannot hide the eventual truth of their actual skill levels within the context of a carefully mentored, collaboratively developed, diverse compilation of exhibits tied to reflective commentary and judgment. The more angles from which we view learning, the better we see it, and that is the virtue of collaborative portfolio development.

Selectivity

The concrete evidence of learning in a portfolio is collected selectively in an appendix of materials which meets the specific purposes of the portfolio. The representation of student work, or products, in the appendix is linked to the reflective component of the learning portfolio, its critical process, and driven by purpose and audience. For example, Table 3.1 suggests some representative ways in which the purpose of a learning portfolio strongly determines the themes of the reflective narrative as well as the types of evidence selected in the appendices.

The examples given, of course, do not exhaust the numerous possibilities across disciplines of how learning portfolios can help students make connections among the purposes, goals, actual experiences, and outcomes of their learning. In fact, Campbell, Cignetti, Melenyzer, Nettles, and Wyman (2001), writing for teacher-preparation candidates seeking professional employment, offer many of the same items listed above but include other potential artifacts that may support a student portfolio. While their items are most relevant to a particular field, a little ingenuity can uncover multiple adaptations to other disciplines. Here are a few from their list:

- Article summaries or critiques
- Case studies
- Classroom learning philosophy and work strategies
- Community service learning activities
- Cooperative learning log
- Field trip journal
- Individualized career plan
- Media competencies

Table 3.1

Purpose, Themes, and Evidence of a Learning Portfolio

Purpose	Themes	Evidence
Improvement	Development, reflective inquiry, focus on goals, philosophy of learning	Drafts, journals, online threaded discussion, emails, statement of goals, classroom assessments, research notes
Job Search	Career preparation, versatile skills, ambitions, potential for future contributions, flexibility	Showcase projects, writing and communication samples, résumé, references, internship evaluations, certifications, reports/logs, computer programs, awards, transcripts
Writing	Voice, creativity, diverse and flexible skills, craftsmanship, facility with language, research proficiency	Essay drafts, journal, listserv or threaded discussion entries, research paper, publications, concept maps or outlines
Prior Learning	Mastery of content	Products demonstrating skills and competency, references, achievement/placement test scores, interview transcript
Problem Solving	Critical thinking, creativity, application of knowledge, flexibility, curiosity	Problem-solving log, lab reports, computer programs, spreadsheet data analyses
Field Experiences	Application of knowledge, trained skills, adaptability	Field journals, logs, reports, video/audio tapes, photos, project leader's evaluation, grant proposal, publication

One other suggestion for addressing the topic of selectivity in gathering the evidence necessary for a sound learning portfolio is, once again, to turn to the proven work of the teaching portfolio movement. Seldin (1993, 1997), for instance, maintains that documentation gathered to support the reflective portion of a faculty portfolio must come as evenly as possible from the three broad areas of 1) information from self, 2) information from others, and 3) products of effective teaching. With only slight modifications, the guidelines are applicable to learning portfolios, reminding us of the importance of both coherence and diversity in balancing the reflective dimension of a portfolio with the numerous and varied artifacts in the appendix. Using the three areas as a framework, students, too, for example, can develop three basic dimensions of their learning portfolios:

- *Information from self*—reflective narratives, personal learning goals, career plan.

- *Information from others*—feedback and evaluations from faculty, recommendation letters, statements from advisors, academic awards, scholarships, undergraduate research grants.

- *Products*—samples of selected work and achievements appropriate for the purpose of the portfolio.

Standards Versus Standardization in Documentation

When gathering the evidence necessary in documenting the sources, extent, meaning, and value of learning in a portfolio, the student and collaborative mentor inevitably will confront the issue of what criteria to use in selecting information for inclusion in the appendices. Students must decide how much and what kinds of documentation to attach to a portfolio, taking into consideration the purpose of the portfolio and the intended audience. They need to reckon with the internal as well as external motivations for developing a learning portfolio and with two interconnected questions: 1) What standards should be used to help focus the scope and shape the unity of the portfolio? 2) How should the portfolio be standardized (or should it be standardized?) for reliability of assessment outcomes?

Recalling the admonitions of Brookfield (1995) and others about the importance of supplying students with clear goals, guidelines, and rubrics for the challenges of systematic reflective inquiry, the problem of standards versus standardization raises a provocative debate over the fundamental rationale for portfolios. For example, Murphy (1997) follows the lead of several scholars and practitioners in arguing that portfolios offer an alternative, individualistic means of evaluating students' learning:

> Portfolios . . . seem to provide the ideal recipe for educational reform because they offer new, more individualized modes of instruction, and because they promise to capture information not easily assessed by other methods. We can use portfolios, for example, to assess students' ability to think critically, articulate and solve complex problems, work collaboratively, conduct research, accomplish long-term, worthwhile projects, and set their own goals for learning. . . . We can use portfolios to assess progress over

time and to assess performance under a variety of conditions and task requirements. (p. 72)

Portfolios should be flexible and dynamic without the homogenizing
effect of standardization to achieve "traditional statistical kinds of reliability" (p. 72).

Williams (2000), on the other hand, concedes that "standardization is
not the same thing as standards" but reasons that we should not ignore "the
fact that standardization is a necessary factor in establishing standards
because it allows for the comparisons that underlie all standards. Rejecting
standardization, therefore, commonly results in a failure of standards"
(p. 136).

Sunstein (2000) counters with a contention that "by privileging the
surface features" and placing too much emphasis on standardization of style
and form in students' learning portfolios, we "create a demand for a superfi-
cial kind of product . . . using curriculum guidelines to shape student texts
and ideas." She reinforces her point with this thought: "It is chilling to
think of the expression 'Beware of what you ask for because you just might
get it' in relationship to our traditional assessment practices . . ." (p. 13).

One potential solution to the quandary of standards versus standardization in the creation and assessment of learning portfolios is to require all
portfolios to share a common set of standards for both content and format
but allow each student the individual, creative opportunity to add a prescribed limit of additional elements that capture the exclusive dimensions
of a particular student's learning experience. The suggestion assumes, of
course, that the portfolio will have an external audience, a condition that
makes some degree of standardization practical and helpful. By combining
prescribed content and format features with individually relevant components, the learning portfolio—especially when produced with the guidance
of a mentor—meets the challenge of standardization for reliable assessment
and honors the individuality of the learner and the imperative of personal
or collective standards in the process of learning.

COLLABORATION AND MENTORING

All of the models described in Part II highlight the way in which student
portfolios have traditionally incorporated, to differing degrees, the fundamental features of reflection and evidence. The role and involvement of the
mentor is less clear, but remember that the value of collaboration in constructing knowledge takes many forms, though the common denominator,

as Bruffee (1993) has shown, is a reconceptualizing of the authority of knowledge, resulting essentially in a student-centered classroom in which learning is a shared endeavor, the effort of a learning community. Thus, while collaboration and mentoring may not be overt facets of a portfolio project, intentionally identified in the design and written into specified goals, the very nature of portfolio development—with its premium on reflection, sharing of evidential materials, and decentralization of the class-room—presupposes a sense of authorship which suggests audience. Whether that audience is a history class engaged in the continuous dis-course of an online threaded discussion, a peer reviewer in a composition course, a teacher providing formative feedback on a business plan assign-ment, a team of lab partners, or a program advisor, the portfolio author is keenly aware of the other as presence, as collaborator. There is even a sense in which, when a learner is strongly self-aware and highly skilled at reflec-tive inquiry, the purportedly private venture of reflective thinking for one-self still invokes an other, the critical self as collaborator.

The teacher who facilitates the portfolio-centered class is inevitably a collaborative mentor just by virtue of privileging a community of reflective practice in which the authority of knowledge as a traditional, static mono-lith gives way to interdependent, active learning or intellectual journeying that stems from reflective thought. Portfolio authors and mentors conse-quently depend on each other to sustain the dynamism of the reflective classroom and the portfolio project. Learning portfolios foster a version of what Dewey (1910) calls "consecutive discourse" and "systematic reflection" (p. 185), or what Brookfield (1995) calls "systematic inquiry" (p. 39); hence, the instructor becomes a genuine teacher (to draw on Dewey's subtle distinction), a mentor who exerts an indelible influence on the student's continual progress of learning and who shares in the construction of that learning.

The faculty member as mentor who helps guide the development of a learning portfolio is a model that is common and natural enough to embrace. The faculty mentor can be the classroom teacher, an academic advisor, a program director, or other faculty member who can help coach the student's portfolio development. More challenging, though potentially no less productive and transformative, is rallying students as collaborators in the processes of discovering a learning philosophy or educational plan, assembling relevant and representative products of learning, reflecting on immediate or long-range learning activities, and evaluating the nature and value of learning experiences. Pixley, in this volume, provides a description of how student portfolio consultants and career advisors (upper-class peer student mentors) have helped shape the formidable Kalamazoo College portfolio project. Also, Herteis, in this volume, suggests the power of teaming fourth-year and third-year students in the portfolio program of the College of Pharmacy and Nutrition at the University of Saskatchewan in Canada.

Another model is to adapt the commonly used Small Group Instructional Diagnosis (SGID) process in such a way to engage students in small group, reflective conversations not about instructional performance but about their own learning experience (see Black, 1998, for a brief summary of the SGID method). A student consultant/collaborator can help peers delve into their learning by posing critical questions to the group about what, how, when, and why they have learned and then asking students to write a thoughtful list of recommendations they might have for self-improvement and for creating a stronger learning environment. The writing can be included in a portfolio and shared in further mentoring sessions with the teacher or with other students in a learning community. Such peer collaboration, support, and encouragement to think across disciplines about one's learning can be a powerful boost to development of higher-level, metacognitive skills and to the concept of learning as community.

Yet another model is that described by Wright and Barton (2001) in a summary of Dalhousie University's successful career portfolio program (see Hung, this volume). Students enroll in credit courses to train as mentors, learning about communication concepts and mentoring skills, career development theory, role playing, conflict resolution, group dynamics, and leadership skills. The authors offer a special directive derived from their experiences over two years of working with student portfolio mentors: "We cannot overemphasize the absolute necessity of thorough preparation and training for student mentors. The preparation includes development of knowledge in the area of career orientations as well as knowledge of the communications process" (p. 70). The positive outcomes of such a mentoring program are evident in the responses given by students about the value of portfolios in helping them not only prepare for jobs but deepen their learning through structured reflection and supportive peer mentoring. As the authors reveal,

> When asked what they liked best about the course, students identified the production of the portfolio itself, the opportunity for self-reflection and growth, and the inter-

action with the professors and their peers. The students identified five key skills learned in the class: personal reflection, goal setting, teamwork, effective listening, and time management. (p. 70)

Dalhousie's peer mentoring program for developing career portfolios is a showcase model that demonstrates how students can be employed to help enrich learning and provide the collaboration, objective perspective, and encouragement needed for producing and maintaining a sound learning portfolio. In concluding their piece, Wright and Barton share several tips for replicating their success on an institutional level:

- Establish a broad-based task force to discuss implementation . . . and seek early input from all potential stakeholders.

- Look to the instructional development center (or committee) on campus for resources.

- Survey faculty to discover who might have already used peer mentoring or student portfolios in their classrooms. Invite them to join the committee or to make presentations on their experiences.

- Seek out expertise in the student services department regarding . . . portfolio writing, and student mentoring.

- Be prepared to patiently explain the peer mentoring concept so that the community supports the project.

- If academic credit for portfolio writing and mentoring is not provided, devise some other form of recognition or compensation in order to attract students. (pp. 73–74)

In a classroom situation, peer mentors may be instructor-assigned or self-selected classmates whose role is to encourage reflection and assist in purposeful selection of supportive evidence to document learning. Such relationships can be the result of cooperative learning groups established at the beginning of a course, and the thoughtful instructor will develop clear expectations and guidelines for both the peer mentors and their portfolio partners. Outside the classroom, peer mentors may be veteran majors in a discipline or alumnae of particular courses or programs. More than just a traditional tutor in a content area, a peer portfolio mentor, especially with some training, offers a balanced, critical perspective on the learning process itself and joins with other students (and the teacher) in creating a community of reflective learners through the shared act of developing learning portfolios.

The chief point of mentoring as a crucial dimension of portfolios is that regardless of who serves as mentor—teacher, advisor, peer—such collaboration, as Hutchings (1990) suggests, results in the conversation and debate needed for human judgment and meaning making:

> Who should be part of that conversation? Much depends
> on purposes, but fruitful things would surely happen
> around a table that included the student—let's say a psy-
> chology major—his department advisor, a faculty member
> from his support area in philosophy, and the director of
> student services with whom he's been working on a peer-
> advising project. (p. 7)

Collaboration may even be as loose as an interactive, web-based set of goals, directions, advice, and models developed as a virtual mentor or guide to portfolio development. One example is the online guide crafted by the University of Lethbridge, Alberta, for both preprofessional student teachers and faculty (http://www.edu.uleth.ca/fe/ppd/contents.html). The particular value of engaging students in the process of collaboration, working in concert with the teacher and helping each other in designing and revising learning portfolios, is summed up again by Hutchings (1990):

> [W]here students are active partners in the assembly and
> analysis of portfolios, they can learn a great deal from the
> method—about putting pieces together, making connec-
> tions, the need for revision, setting goals for the future....
> [W]hat's most at stake here are educational values. Choos-
> ing portfolios is choosing to enact—and communicate to
> students—a view of learning as involving, personal, con-
> nected, and ongoing. (p. 8)

4

Electronic Learning Portfolios

ELECTRONIC PORTFOLIOS

The advent of digital technology has done much to alter the way in which learning is displayed, shared, and analyzed in multimedia and hypermedia environments. The varied accounts of uses of electronic portfolios in Part II and the diverse models in Parts III and IV of this volume provide compelling evidence of the increasing popularity of electronic portfolios as a powerful method of enhancing and assessing student learning. Cambridge (2001) and her team of assisting editors invite us "to read about the practices of individuals and institutions" invested in electronic portfolios, imagining, as we study the various cases and models in their volume, "what might be as we move at ever more accelerating rates into new possibilities" (p. *viii*) for using digital technology in portfolio development.

Browsing the American Association for Higher Education's searchable database at the Electronic Portfolio Clearinghouse site (http://www.aahe.org/teaching/portfolio_db.htm) reveals a number of institutional programs that use electronic portfolios to foster students' reflection and to assess and evaluate learning. The list includes colleges and universities as diverse as Elmhurst and Messiah, Dartmouth, Kalamazoo, Indiana University, Amsterdam Faculty of Education (Netherlands), GateWay Community College, Rose-Hulman Institute of Technology, and University of Florida, among others. Clearly, for students and faculty increasingly proficient in the ubiquitous technologies that have challenged and redefined traditional pedagogies, reshaping K–12 and higher education in our time, the electronic portfolio is an exciting and effective tool for improving, assessing, and evaluating learning.

Defining the Electronic Portfolio

What exactly is an electronic portfolio? Answers vary as considerably as they do in defining print portfolios because of the many purposes for which portfolios are developed and the multiple technologies available. Kaufman and Jafari (2002) of CyberLab at Indiana University–Purdue University Indianapolis surveyed an assortment of educators to gather definitions, and the wide range of responses is available online.

One definition is offered by the Alphabet Superhighway, a K–12 initiative of the US Department of Education, a reminder that portfolios—even the electronic varieties—have enjoyed considerable attention in the grade schools. The definition, available online at http://www.ash.udel.edu /ash/teacher/portfolio.html, is just as applicable to college-level portfolios; its central message is that electronic innovations enhance the virtue of portfolios in representing a learning history.

ADVANTAGES OF ELECTRONIC PORTFOLIOS

The same site above also provides a useful set of advantages to electronic portfolios, summarized in the following list:

- Electronic portfolios foster active learning.

- Electronic portfolios motivate students.

- Electronic portfolios are instruments of feedback.

- Electronic portfolios are instruments of discussion on student performance.

- Electronic portfolios exhibit benchmark performance.

- Electronic portfolios are accessible.

- Electronic portfolios can store multiple media.

- Electronic portfolios are easy to upgrade.

- Electronic portfolios allow cross-referencing of student work.

Electronic media choices have introduced an array of strategies for archiving, organizing, and reflecting on information about a student's learning. Using hypertext links, for example, students can present and explore multiple layers of accessible documentary information in a way that reinforces the notion of learning as a shared, interactive process, inviting both the portfolio author and audience progressively deeper and wider into the constructed process of learning. Also, because web portfolio projects, especially, often make much or all of the student's work publicly accessible online, the electronic portfolio heightens what Yancey (2001) calls the "social action" and "interactivity" (p. 20) of learning. Sometimes, electronic portfolios are not posted as web pages but presented instead on conventional floppy disk, Zip disk, or CD-ROM (see Holt and McAllister in this volume). Such mediums also facilitate the shared dimension of learning in a way that is less cumbersome and more instant than hard-copy pages and folders.

DISADVANTAGES OF ELECTRONIC PORTFOLIOS

The versatility of electronic portfolios in providing a high-tech means of collecting and storing information is intriguing but also problematic because of the often daunting amount of training necessary, the potentially confusing variety of hardware and software choices available, and the dizzying pace at which technology evolves. Springfield (2001), for example, mentions such barriers, commenting on problems encountered with numerous products. Barrett (2000a) reviews the advantages and limitations of common technologies for portfolio building. Lankes (1995) also points out various approaches to digitizing portfolios, referring to how some educators have had to develop customized templates for easier implementation of portfolios for assessment and career preparation.

Transferability of files from one type of computer program to another is an additional worry. Barrett's (2000c) solution is to use Adobe Acrobat PDF (Portable Document Format) files as the ideal medium for electronic portfolio development because of its user-friendly ability to cross many platforms and applications.

The National Education Association (2000–2001), taking into consideration the potential hurdles in moving from print to digital portfolio formats, issues the following cautions in its web site on portfolio assessment:

Bits & Bytes Advice

Data in digital form can easily be cross-referenced, overlaid, and analyzed.... If you want to take advantage of technological tools to create electronic portfolios, you should consider several factors, however, before you make a change from a traditional system:

• **Access.** The hardware and software used to capture and store the student portfolios must be accessible to both teacher and students. If your computers, scanner, and printer are still down the hall in the Computer Lab, this may not be the time to initiate electronic portfolios.

- **High-end Tools.** Depending on the subject matter, you'll want to be able to store multiple data sources (text, voice, video, image, etc.). The capacity to store more than a single file format will also give a more well-rounded representation of the student's work. Therefore, you will need access to at least one high-end workstation with scanner, OCR (optical character recognition) software, printer, and perhaps digital camera.

- **Space.** Graphics and photographic images take up a great deal more system storage than text does. Be sure that your school's system can support large files without compromising other applications. You may also want to develop a regular schedule of backing up files and archiving outdated material to magnetic tape or CD-ROM storage to avoid an unnecessary drain on your system or the loss of vital material.

- **Labor.** Accumulating information for an electronic portfolio is both labor-intensive and time-consuming. Although you may delegate this task to each student as part of his or her role in compiling a portfolio, always be careful to stay on top of the process.

- **Administration.** Before starting, determine how you will administer the electronic portfolios. You will want a database application that establishes an area for each student, stores various file formats, and allows for annotated comments appended to each item. You may also want a tool with security features and password protection, so that the privacy of portfolios cannot be compromised. You'll also want to make sure that the interface (ease of use, appearance, etc.) is "friendly" and appealing to both yourself and your students.

- **Hybrid Solutions.** More often than not, portfolios are the composite of evaluation techniques, including standardized testing, completed assignments, original works, teacher comments, student reflections, and peer reviews. You may not want—or be able—to capture all of these products into the electronic portfolio, so you should try

to develop portfolio content on the basis of your identified goals and the needs of your students.

The assessment portfolio—whether electronic or paper-
based—is intended to document student learning and
progress, as well as allow students to identify their own
goals and accomplishments. Technology can be a poweful
tool in your use of this instrument. (pp. 1–2)

Young (2002) reports on several responses to such issues. One is a consortium (http://www.eportconsortium.org) formed by the Indiana University–Purdue University Indianapolis and the University of California, Los
Angeles to develop e-portfolio software that, for an institutional membership fee, "will give students and advisers tools to build portfolios" (Young,
2002, p. A32). Another consortium is affiliated with the National Learning
Infrastructure Initiative of EDUCAUSE (http://www.educause.edu/nlii),
and it consists of institutions from several states—including California,
Massachusetts, Minnesota, and Washington—all attempting to make the
process of developing electronic portfolios more cost and labor efficient
with the positive outcome of enhanced student learning.

FUNDAMENTALS

The landscape of portfolio development has expanded astonishingly with
the advent of multimedia and hypermedia. Yet, though the mediums have
changed from print on paper to electronic hypertext, the fundamental
process of learning portfolio development remains steadfast. Cambridge
(2001) points out that reflection is central to learning, and the reflective
core of sound learning portfolios is what transforms mere accumulated
information to meaningful knowledge, an idea I mentioned earlier. Yancey
(2001) follows up with the assertion that "electronic portfolios are created
through the same basic processes used for print portfolios: collection, selection, and reflection" (p. 20).

In the interest of clarifying the deep purposes and value of creating
electronic portfolios and keeping a premium on meaningful reflection and
careful, strategic implementation, Yancey (2001) shares the following
heuristic, further developed in her text, for effective design and creation of
student electronic portfolios:

• What is/are the purpose/s?

- How familiar is the portfolio concept? Is the familiarity a plus or a minus?

- Who wants to create an electronic portfolio, and why?

- Why electronic? What about electronic is central to the model? And is sufficient infrastructure (resources, knowledge, commitment) available for the electronic portfolio?

- What processes are entailed? What resources are presumed?

- What faculty development component does the model assume or include?

- What skills will students need to develop?

- What curricular enhancement does the model assume or include?

- How will the portfolio be introduced?

- How will the portfolio be reviewed? (pp. 84–86)

Having reflected carefully on the issues raised in the heuristic, one can then proceed to more detailed questions of implementation and use. Yancey (2001) follows with an expanded list of recommendations for setting up an electronic portfolio program. Here is a summary of her tips:

- Think rhetorically. Who is creating the portfolio and why? Who is reading it and why?

- Consider how the electronic portfolio needs to be electronic. How will it be interactive? What relationships and connections does the digital form make possible?

- Consider how the portfolio will be interactive socially.

- Develop some key terms that you can associate with your model of an e-portfolio, and use them consistently.

- Be realistic about how long it will take to introduce the model and the skills that faculty and students will need.

- Be realistic about the difficulty that teachers may have in designing reflective texts, that students may experience in writing reflections, and that teachers may have in responding to and evaluating those reflections.

- Perhaps more than other innovative practices, the development of e-portfolios calls for a collaborative process of development. (pp. 86–87)

SELECTED RESOURCES

The amount of information on electronic portfolios available online is staggering. A simple query on a standard Internet search engine produces over a half-million sites, though not all are relevant to higher education; many are K–12 projects, student samples, commercial ventures, or simply inoperative links. Here are just a few that may prove useful, listed alphabetically:

- Albion College Digital Portfolio site with extensive information, template, student samples: http://www.albion.edu/digitalportfolio

- Alverno College Diagnostic Digital Portfolio. Password protected information but brief details available: http://www.alverno.edu/academics/ddp.html

- Helen Barrett's educational and entrepreneurial e-portfolio site with many links to information, guidelines, resources: http://electronic port folios.com

- California State University, Los Angeles, Webfolio Project with information, student samples: http://www.calstatela.edu/academic/webfolio

- "Creating an Electronic Portfolio" site includes links to resources and rudimentary information on process, evaluation rubric: http:// cte.jhu.edu/techacademy/fellows/Spencer/webquest/lasindex.html

- Dartmouth College electronic Career Services Portfolio site: http://www.dartmouth.edu/~csrc/portfolio/index.html

- GateWay Community College, Maricopa, e-portfolio information: http://www.gwc.maricopa.edu/class/e-portfolio/index.html

- Kalamazoo College portfolio page with extensive links to e-portfolio information, student samples: http://www.kzoo.edu/pfolio/index.html

- LaGuardia Community College's site with many links to information, guidelines, resources, student samples: http://www.eportfolio.lagcc.cuny.edu

- Ohio University e-portfolio site with extensive information, guidelines, instructions: http://www.cob.ohiou.edu/~mgt300/esp/portfolio.htm

- Seton Hall University samples of teacher education e-portfolios: http://education.shu.edu/portfolios

- St. Olaf College's Web Portfolios site with extensive information about educational purpose, goals, guidelines, templates, models: http://www.stolaf.edu/depts/cis/web_portfolios.htm

- Stanford University Learning Laboratory E-Folio project site with brief information about Stanford's prototype of "electronic knowledge database": http://sll.stanford.edu/consulting/tools/efolio

- Tidewater Community College, Donna Reiss's Webfolio Project with templates, resources, student samples: http://www.wordsworth2.net/webfolio/index.htm

- University of Florida e-portfolio information, templates, student samples: http://www.coe.ufl.edu/school/portfolio

- University of Pennsylvania e-portfolio site with information, guidelines, content and design strategies, resources: http://www.upenn.edu/careerservices/college/electronic_portfolio.html

- University of South Dakota Technology Literacy Center e-portfolio site, offering guidelines, do's and don'ts, common problems: http://www.usd.edu/tlc/eportfolio

- University of Virginia, Curry School of Education portfolio information with links to student samples: http://curry.edschool.virginia.edu/curry/class/edlf/589-07/sample.html

- University of Wisconsin, Superior, e-portfolio information, guidelines, with available manual in MS Word: http://www2.uwsuper.edu/assessment

- Utah State University Digital Portfolio Project site with extensive information, links to grade schools using e-portfolios, student samples: http://myfolio.usu.edu

- Valdosta State University e-portfolio page with links to PowerPoint information, student samples: http://chiron.valdosta.edu/coeadvising/professional_portfolio.htm

- Virginia Wesleyan College e-portfolio information, student samples: http://www.vwc.edu/academics/portfolio/

- Wesleyan University's site for electronic portfolios used for advisement: https://portfolio2.wesleyan.edu/names.nsf?login

THE LINK TO LEARNING

According to Cambridge (2001), technology, as it turns out, is "only one component of decision-making about the use of electronic portfolios and . . . not the most crucial one" (p. 11). The real link to promoting learning with portfolios, regardless of the technologies pressed into service, is holding fast to the fundamentals. Discerning the foundational value of portfolios underneath the technology, Yancey (2001) puts it this way:

> [M]ore generally, portfolios bring with them three key characteristics:
>
> • They function as a means of both review and planning.
>
> • They are social in nature.
>
> • They are grounded in reflection (p. 19).

The key elements of effective portfolio projects, then, as identified in Chapter 3, remain the most salient issues in portfolio development:

• Reflection

• Evidence

• Collaboration and mentoring

Just as in teaching portfolios (Seldin, 1993, 1997), these three dimensions are the most strongly determining factors in successful use of learning portfolios, whether the format is print or electronic. When all three components are present in the process of constructing, reviewing, and revising the portfolio, student learning is richer, more lasting, and more transformative. We will then have realized the full, authentic value of the learning portfolio.

Part II

Models of Successful Use
of Learning Portfolios

The following contributors present a collection of models of successful use of both print and electronic learning portfolios. The variety of models suggests the many ways in which learning portfolios are adapted across purposes, disciplines, programs, and institutions. The diverse models of portfolio implementation offer both theoretical ideas and practical information, and readers are encouraged to consider what would work for them individually to improve student learning.

Tanya Augsburg
The Personal, the Educational, and the Professional:
Incorporating the Learning Portfolio Into the Curriculum
in the BIS Program at Arizona State University

Lisa Batterbee and Andrew Dunham
Four Years of Reflection:
The Digital Portfolio Project at Albion College

Vicki Bocchicchio
The Senior Honors Portfolio
Kent State University

David G. Brown and H. David Womack
Persuasion, Politics, Pragmatics, and the Student Portfolio Movement
Wake Forest University

Earl B. Brown, Jr.
Demonstrating Mastery Through an Honors Portfolio
Radford University

Jená A. Burges
Changing How Students Think About Writing:
The Web-Based Learning Environment Project Portfolio
Longwood College

Candee C. Chambers
Portfolios Within an Honors Program:
The Honors Preparation Year and Beyond
Mercyhurst College

L. Dee Fink
Learning Portfolios:
A Powerful Tool for Enhancing Course Design
University of Oklahoma

Eileen Herteis
Experiential Learning Portfolios in Professional Programs:
A Canadian Perspective
University of Saskatchewan

Dennis M. Holt and Paula McAllister
Using Electronic Portfolios for the Improvement of
Teaching and Learning
University of North Florida

Jeanette Hung
Portfolio Design:
The Basics
Dalhousie University

Randall L. Kolar and David A. Sabatini
Use of Reflective Writing/Learning Portfolios in a Junior-Level
Water Resources Engineering Class
University of Oklahoma

Ted Panitz
The Math Student Course Portfolio
Cape Cod Community College

Zaide Pixley
The Kalamazoo Portfolio
Kalamazoo College

Farland Stanley
Increasing Student Comprehension Through
Learning Portfolios in Archaeology:
The Case of Caesarea Maritima in Israel
University of Oklahoma

David A. Thomas
Interdisciplinary Effectiveness and the Learning Portfolio:
Developing the Transferable Skills Required in the
21st Century Workplace
Arizona State University

Catherine M. Wehlburg
The General Education Portfolio at Stephens College

The Personal, the Educational, and the Professional: Incorporating the Learning Portfolio Into the Curriculum in the BIS Program at Arizona State University

Tanya Augsburg
Arizona State University

BACKGROUND OF BIS

The portfolio-based Bachelor of Interdisciplinary Studies (BIS) was created in 1997 as Arizona State University's (ASU) response to nontraditional student needs. With the inception of the degree, BIS majors take six courses in two concentration areas and four core courses. Because the BIS degree was so new, the university-wide advisory committee that designed it instilled two precautionary measures within the degree. The first was that one of the courses, BIS 401, would be an applied interdisciplinary studies or internship course that was both practical and academic as it required a research component. The second was that the BIS degree would be a portfolio-based program requiring its students to track their progress throughout their education.

Initially, the advisory committee envisioned that the BIS program would remain small with 400 students projected by 1999. By fall 2001 there were approximately 1,500 BIS majors. I believe there are three primary reasons for the BIS degree's unexpected success, and all three can be linked to the portfolio requirement.

Reasons for the Success of the BIS

The BIS portfolio. The first reason students are attracted to the degree is precisely the BIS portfolio. BIS faculty generally regard the portfolio primarily as a pedagogical tool that helps students to identify values, interests, goals, skills, and specific types of knowledge. Students tend to view the portfolio more as a tool for self-legitimization. The BIS portfolio enables students to demonstrate with artifacts and reflection exercises what they have learned and focused on throughout their education. More specifically, by integrating the personal, the educational, and the professional by means of the portfolio assignment, BIS students can exhibit how the skills and knowledge they have learned in the classroom, in their extracurricular activities, in their internships, and in their work experience transfer to skills required for their chosen career. In effect, BIS students consider the portfolio as a personal marketing tool that is essential for life after graduation, whether they plan to apply to graduate school or enter the job market. Not surprisingly, many BIS majors enter the program believing that the portfolio will help them be better prepared for and more confident of their lives after graduation.

The value of cross-training. Second, BIS students recognize the value of cross-training in one's education for career preparation. The majority of students at ASU are employed, so they know on a practical level that they need to cross-train. Students realize that in today's world many jobs require knowledge in more than one area as well as versatility in applying that knowledge. BIS students use their portfolios to document their cross-training experience, which can include instances of working in interdisciplinary projects and/or teams.

The internship. Third, the uniqueness of the internship experience gained in BIS 401, the applied interdisciplinary studies course, makes it especially attractive to students. Students gain crucial professional experience by means of experiential learning; they have to document their activities and conduct academic research on their learning sites. By the time they complete their portfolios, BIS students learn not only how to conceptualize their experiential learning experiences but how to articulate them in both professional and scholarly manners.

Faculty have learned how to implement portfolios into the BIS curriculum through a partnership with Career Services, a collaboration that has been critical for the development of the portfolio assignment and the program as a whole. The BIS program, its faculty, and its students continue to benefit from the ongoing partnership with Career Services.

ONE BIS FACULTY MEMBER'S PERSPECTIVE

To be perfectly honest, I was unfamiliar with student learning portfolios until I began teaching in the BIS program during the summer of 1998. In late spring 1998, a workshop served as the BIS faculty's crash course in student portfolios, preparing faculty to explain the theory and rationale behind portfolios to students. ASU Career Services staff members present two portfolio workshops in BIS classes. An introductory workshop in BIS 301 focuses on portfolios as a place for storing artifacts and describes various types of portfolios. While students are introduced to the idea that there are many different types of portfolios, the type of portfolio Career Services emphasizes is the personal discovery portfolio since personal discovery is the first step in the career development process. The introductory workshop also addresses organization strategies: For example, should students organize their portfolios according to chronology or to skills they have been obtaining? The workshop stresses skills; one activity, for example, involves students' breaking down into groups and making lists of skills for various types of activities. Students are always amazed to learn how many skills they learn from their freshman composition class as well as from waiting tables. The workshop introduces the concepts of artifacts and includes activities that facilitate active learning where students decide for themselves what constitutes an appropriate artifact for inclusion in their portfolios.

Overall, the introductory portfolio workshop has been effective in introducing the idea of portfolios to BIS students. But because the portfolio objectives for the BIS program go beyond personal discovery and career planning to include educational issues, the portfolios that students establish in both BIS 301 and the senior seminar, BIS 402, are in fact hybrid portfolios. In BIS 301 the student portfolio is a combination of the personal discovery, education, and career planning portfolio. In BIS 402, there is a shift of emphasis, as the personal discovery elements are minimized and the education and career planning elements are underscored. Hence, I have begun to supplement the career service portfolio workshops with my own material. In the following sections I relate how I approach the BIS 301 and BIS 402 assignments and the BIS 402 electronic portfolio option.

BIS 301 PORTFOLIO ASSIGNMENT

I begin explaining the BIS portfolio assignment by describing the five types of portfolios helpful to college students: the personal discovery portfolio, the education portfolio, the career development portfolio, the showcase portfolio, and the electronic portfolio. Each portfolio conveys a different message.

After providing some historical background regarding portfolios and some context to the growing trend of the portfolio professional, I give strict guidelines on how the portfolios look. Fifty percent of the BIS portfolio assignment grade is based on content while the other 50% is based on presentation. I instruct students that because the portfolio is a representation of themselves and how they view their education, nothing less than an excellent effort is acceptable. Once the students realize that the portfolio assignment makes sense, not only does any student resistance disappear, but enthusiasm for doing the assignment abounds.

To ensure an even playing field, I provide a list of required and optional elements for the BIS 301 portfolio. I ascertain that even students with little or no work or other related experience can receive an excellent grade on their portfolios. Required elements include a large three-ring binder, dividers, and plastic sheet covers to protect pages. Other required elements include a title page; table of contents; thoughtful mission statement; certain ASU-specific advising documents, such as a declaration of major (DOG) and a report of students' fulfilled requirements (DARS); and sample work from BIS 301. I also require elements that I have incorporated from Career Services: a values checklist and one-page reflection, general skills list, description of one's five top skills, list of skills one has learned from coursework, and list of skills one has gained from life/work/extracurricular/volunteer activities. I place heavy emphasis on students' being able to recognize their skills and articulate how they have developed them, utilizing concrete examples. I also require BIS students to include a personal strengths and weaknesses inventory.

Additionally, I provide students with eight discovery options, including exercises in personal discovery, academic discovery, professional exploration, and integration. Students can choose any three of the eight options; thus, students decide for themselves in which of the areas they would like to do more investigation.

If students fulfill all of the required and optional elements, the highest grade they can receive is a 95; to receive a 100, they have to provide five elements or artifacts external to the BIS program: sample work from other classes, academic transcripts, write-ups of volunteer work, samples of artwork, awards, certificates of merit, or letters of recommendation. The additional information enables students to express their individuality; while some students create portfolios that have a scrapbook appearance, including photographs and other personal material, others assemble very professional looking portfolios that are straight to the point with no extras. Most students elect to include extras whenever possible.

BIS 402 Portfolio Assignment

In BIS 402, the senior capstone seminar course, students are asked to revisit the portfolios they created in BIS 301. Often, BIS 402 is the last course students take before graduation. For BIS 402, Career Services offers a second portfolio workshop, emphasizing the showcase portfolio and how to incorporate it in job interviews. I additionally assign a practice session in which students first describe a scenario (who the audience is, what job they are applying for) and then deliver a presentation similar to one they would give during a job interview. If a student is applying to graduate school, the audience becomes an admissions committee.

The BIS 402 Electronic Portfolio Option

The BIS portfolio requirement has posed some unforeseen challenges for online students. The majority of online students take the course locally. Most of them can drop off and pick up their portfolios without any problems. Some online students elect to take the senior seminar elsewhere. To require out-of-state students to send thick BIS 402 portfolios via overnight mail and to provide me with the return postage would be an expensive proposition and almost punitive. Thus, I have given students the alternative of developing their portfolios electronically. Electronic portfolios are fantastic for job searching but admittedly remain problematic due to security and privacy issues. Some students opt to create electronic portfolios only for their assignments, while others incorporate them in their career hunts. I advise students to give out the URLs for their electronic portfolios sparingly as anyone could download their documents.

Overall, students have been enthusiastic about creating electronic portfolios and have succeeded in creating attractive portfolios quickly even with little or no previous web page design experience. Currently, numerous free sites on the web permit students to create their own home pages with easily linked documents. While security issues are extremely problematic, students express a tremendous sense of accomplishment from creating a complex and professional looking web site about themselves for the first time.

Evaluating Student Portfolios

Part IV of this book includes labeled samples of my evaluation forms for the BIS 301 and BIS 402 electronic portfolio assignments. I distribute the forms to students prior to the assignment due dates. The checklist format of the evaluation forms helps students fulfill the requirements and allows for quick but thorough grading, which is essential for faculty members in the BIS program, who average 90 to 110 students per semester.

BIS STUDENT TESTIMONIALS

Students often tell me in person the successes they have with portfolios. Occasionally, students send me emails about their experiences with portfolios. I quote from two without comment, the first from a BIS 301 student in summer 2001, the second from a BIS 402 student in summer 1999:

> In BIS 301, the most influential and rewarding project was the portfolio. It allowed me as a person, and as a student, to portray areas in my life and characteristics about myself, that I was most proud of, and it also helped me to market my areas of emphasis, so that potential employers will be able to spot my talent/strengths more efficiently and faster, compared to a regular application and résumé. The portfolio assignment will be kept with me for a long time to come, and it will be used until I am settled in a profession that I know I will be involved in for a long time. I found out more about myself within that week of working on the portfolio than I have my whole life. It FORCED me to strain, stretch, and search for qualities that I wouldn't have acknowledged beforehand. It was a growing experience that has helped me in getting a job in only a few weeks after the class ended.

> I wanted to email you sooner, but I had two more interviews yesterday, and I did another presentation too. Over the summer my first presentation went very well. I presented the portfolio and gave my speech. . . . They were very impressed with the speech as well as the portfolio. They commented on the style, organization, and content of the portfolio. The vice president also showed the president the portfolio. They both took turns reading excerpts from various papers. They felt it was outstanding that a person could include academic and personal accounts of life events and be able to share them with a complete stranger. This gave them an insight as to who I was and what has happened to me thus far. I interviewed with these individuals for two hours and was offered a job on the

spot. . . . Yesterday I had my second interview for a full-time position and did another portfolio presentation. I presented and gave the speech again. The interviewers were very impressed with the layout of the portfolio, the content, and various quotes I stated in the speech. They said it was very professional. . . . Other co-workers also viewed my portfolio and were fascinated by what I put together and how professional it was. After the interview I was the topic of conversation, as they were very impressed. I hear next week on the full-time position. . . . No matter how much students grumble about the assignment, it is well worth it. I had to start from scratch and was able to put a fabulous portfolio together.

CONCLUSION

The BIS portfolio assignment continues to evolve. Student testimonials such as the two above are extremely helpful to faculty and to the program as a whole. While there is no denying that students like to complain about the assignment's amount of work right before the due date, afterwards, BIS students are typically very appreciative of having had to complete the portfolio. A future research project would conduct surveys sent to BIS graduates to learn how effective BIS student portfolios have been in helping students integrate their education with their personal goals. A personal goal of mine is to write a portfolio textbook for BIS students. Currently, BIS faculty are in the process of designing a student evaluation that will give us more information, both qualitative and quantitative, about the efficacy of the BIS portfolio for student learning. For the time being, BIS faculty continue to rely on overwhelmingly positive student feedback and collaboration with other academic units in further developing BIS learning portfolio assignments.

Four Years of Reflection: The Digital Portfolio Project at Albion College

Lisa Batterbee and Andrew Dunham
Albion College

In the initial stages of development of a comprehensive first-through-senior-year program at Albion College, a theme began to emerge, centering on the connection between students' personal and academic growth and how best to help students explore their personal and educational values and goals. We assumed that while students navigate their way through a myriad of curricular and co-curricular experiences, they need a method to help them put those experiences together in a coherent fashion. Those experiences for the students include in-class and out-of-class experiences; academic, personal, and career planning; the relationship of students' general education courses to their major/concentration/discipline; and multiple-discipline and multiple-inquiry based thinking and analysis.

After two years of planning, we determined that the most appropriate way for students not only to start exploration of values and goals, but also to record, plan, reflect upon, and communicate those values and goals, was through a portfolio maintained throughout their four years at Albion. As such, the portfolio project is an integral part of the first-year experience program.

WHY USE PORTFOLIOS?

The concept of a portfolio program was first discussed early in the development of the comprehensive student program. Portfolios would offer our students the ability to document the connections of their personal and academic lives and function as a tool for communicating what they are learning and planning. The portfolio project is designed so that students understand the power and importance of such a tool and utilize it voluntarily to develop their personal and academic plans as early as possible in their first year. Essentially, the portfolios cover three main areas:

1) Personal/career plan and learning outside the classroom

2) Academic planning and in-class learning

3) Merging the personal and academic plans

PERSONAL/CAREER PLAN AND LEARNING OUTSIDE THE CLASSROOM

Beginning in their first semester, students start to develop a personal plan that leads to the development of a career plan. Students start this process through completion of a self-assessment tool that aids in deepening their understanding of their values, goals, and expectations.

The personal planning process also helps students translate what they are doing outside the classroom into what they are learning. Through the personal planning process, students are able to explain what skills and knowledge they have acquired through their involvement outside of the classroom. Students also learn how best to articulate the skills and knowledge that are transferable to different work or academic environments.

ACADEMIC PLAN AND IN-CLASS LEARNING

During the first year, students develop an academic plan and learn to articulate what they are learning in class. Through their portfolio, students should be able clearly to articulate not only what they have learned in their courses but also how they can apply the different modes of inquiry they experience. The main purpose of the academic portion of the portfolio is to assist the student to become intentional in thinking about and planning his or her academic program and progress. The student should consider important questions: Do I need to complete an internship? Do I want to participate in an off-campus program? What courses will help me increase my historical, scientific, artistic, and cultural perspectives?

MERGING THE PERSONAL AND ACADEMIC PLANS

As students progress from first-year students to seniors, they transform their portfolios to reflect who they are, what they value, and what their plans are. By necessity, the academic plan and personal plan merge to provide a comprehensive overview of the student. Throughout the process, students begin to grow in their own self-knowledge and start to reflect upon their experiences, learning to integrate all experience into a comprehensive summary of knowledge, expertise, abilities, and understanding.

USING DIGITAL PORTFOLIOS

The positive aspects of a digital portfolio seemed to match exactly what the students would need in three very important ways. First, a web-based program would enable students to easily access, modify, and distribute information stored in the portfolio. Students who work with other forms of electronic media can readily merge that work into their portfolios; for example, student-created digital recordings, a work of hypertext, or hypermedia can be added to academic or personal plans. Further, the digital portfolio is easy and inexpensive for students to reproduce as opposed to portfolios that are compiled on traditional media.

Throughout the implementation of the program, we have found that most students are confident with web-based technology and readily adopt the skills required to maintain and update their portfolios. The web-based platform provides students with tremendous flexibility in terms of their ability to modify and change the look and content of their portfolio. The connections between their curricular and co-curricular experiences are not usually manifested in a neat, linear fashion. The digital portfolio is an optimal nonlinear framework from which students can present the connections among these experiences, allowing students better to understand the different intentional and unintentional linkages in their learning process. Also, viewers of the digital portfolio have the freedom to enter and exit from different points in the portfolio while still seeing the overall connectedness of the portfolio.

STARTING THE DIGITAL PORTFOLIO PROJECT: THE FIRST YEAR

To help assure the successful implementation of the digital portfolio project, we determined a need to provide accessible ways to educate students on the development of their portfolios and to help them further develop and reflect on their portfolios during their college career and after graduation. The portfolio project was integrated as a main tenet of the First-Year Experience Program, enabling us to reach all of the first-year students and have First-Year Experience staff and student mentors work directly with students in the development of their portfolios.

We plan for each of the students to attend an initial portfolio training session with their first-year seminar. The training sessions are coordinated and presented by the digital portfolio coordinator, a member of our Information Technology staff. Training focuses on two main learning strategies: 1) having students reflect on themselves, what they have learned, what they want to do with that learning, and how their education is interconnected, and 2) instructing students in how to use web-based media and learn what components are necessary for their digital portfolio.

An Ongoing Process

We expect students to repeat the self-assessment and goal-setting exercises on a semester or annual basis. Reevaluation of their experiences and plans should lead to portfolio revision and growth. Additional training opportunities are offered to help students with content and format and to help them build on their technical skills and abilities.

Students are not left to fend for themselves in the process. Each of the seminar staff and student mentors is also instructed in the development of the digital portfolio and asked to follow the progress of their seminar students' portfolios.

Portfolio Development

In Part IV of this book, we share the portfolio development information that all students are given to aid them in their portfolio development at Albion College. The first exhibit is a section of our web site that helps students focus on self-assessment, goal setting, and making a plan. This section attempts to get the students interested in their portfolio development, allowing them to reflect on what they have done so far and to plan for the future.

The second exhibit reveals how after doing some self-assessment, planning, and goal setting, students then move on to the second phase of development, putting the portfolio together. We advise students to think about their portfolio in two ways: as a file cabinet and a briefcase. The file cabinet serves students by storing all of their private information, such as their self-assessment exercises, goals, objectives, and other items that they don't want to share publicly. The briefcase portion of their portfolio is the public space where students store what they currently want to share with others. Students are encouraged to keep reflective materials from previous stages of development, enabling them to observe and reflect on their personal development and learning.

The second exhibit also provides general descriptions of what might be in students' file cabinet or briefcase. The descriptions cover the first year through the senior year, giving students a starting point for what to include in their portfolios and reminding them of what might be helpful for the public to view. The process effectively represents a student's four years in Albion's successful portfolio development program.

The Senior Honors Portfolio

Vicki Bocchicchio
Kent State University

Seniors at Kent State University's (KSU) Honors College have the option of selecting a one-credit learning portfolio project as their final honors requirement. The senior honors portfolio provides an opportunity for students to review their undergraduate experience and to select from that experience about eight to ten artifacts that provide the best evidence of meeting the following honors college goals:

- Academic excellence
- Campus and community service
- Global awareness
- Appreciation of cultural events and institutions
- Personal growth

A 15- to 25-page reflection paper integrates the collection with the students' current personal observations of educational growth and development. A mentoring instructor guides the portfolio collection and the reflection paper. The student and the instructor are invited to an initial meeting with the Senior Portfolio Review Committee during the first two weeks of the semester to answer any questions and provide any details about the project that are not apparent in the guidelines. The portfolio project culminates with an exit interview with the same portfolio committee; however, the instructor is responsible for final evaluation and grading.

THE CONTENTS OF THE PORTFOLIO

The portfolio collection includes documentation of carefully selected milestones representing meaningful experiences related to honors college values. The guidelines indicate that students may include written, visual, and taped entries among their artifacts. Students are also invited to share evaluations from supervisors of relevant community service or part-time jobs.

The selection of artifacts is left up to the student, with some guidance from the faculty mentor and advisor, but we do expect, of course, that honors work will represent at least a portion of the meaningful experiences of our students. For example, honors classes, individual honors projects, and community service done for honors credit show up in the majority of the completed portfolios. In addition to samples of honors work, portfolios have included photographs from a choreographic project, set designs for theater productions, fashion design sketches, snapshots from study abroad experiences, and articles written for some of our student publications. Because our portfolio stresses reflection, students often include artifacts from their personal lives over the four years, so we have seen letters to and from family members, photographs of close friends, programs and ticket stubs from cultural events, and journal entries.

REFLECTION AND INTEGRATION

The reflective nature of the portfolio is demonstrated in the 15- to 25-page paper that integrates the student's collection of artifacts with a carefully considered evaluation of academic and personal growth. Since the portfolio is a retrospective effort to make meaning of the student's college career, the reflective paper is an overview and critical analysis of that individual's four years of academic experiences. Consequently, the paper often contains highly subjective and personal material. In fact, some of our students have been considerably creative in shaping their reflection paper to fit their personal experiences as an undergraduate. One student walked the reader through a campus tour in her paper, as she made connections to the physical places that symbolized the milestones in her experiences. Another student wrote the paper as a series of letters to the daughter she gave up for adoption years earlier, and yet another imagined that she was writing the paper for her grandchildren. Some students prefer to intersperse reflection with the collection instead of confining it to an introductory essay. However they organize the reflection, we urge them to integrate themes rather than simply follow their semester-by-semester progress.

By emphasizing the integration of the artifacts and the reflection paper, the senior honors portfolio at KSU differs significantly from traditional professional portfolios students often use to supplement their résumés. The audience is not a prospective employer. Traditional portfolios focus on how the reader will measure the student based on the items selected for inclusion, while our portfolio asks the student to take measure of his or her own personal growth and development. Occasionally, a student includes a pre-professional experience as one of the artifacts in the portfolio (an internship or summer job), but these are included as only part of the picture in what we hope is a larger, more holistic self-view. Many students completing the portfolio share with us their exhilaration at deepening their self-awareness or discovering the self-reflective process for the first time.

THE ROLE OF THE FACULTY MENTOR

The role of the faculty mentor or advisor is crucial in this process. Students typically select a faculty advisor who not only is familiar with their best academic work, but also knows and is interested in the student's more general educational goals and activities. The mentor provides the following support:

- Helps the student determine the specific goals of the project
- Reviews artifact items for the final collection
- Discusses the physical layout of the portfolio with the student
- Helps the student identify themes and directions in the work
- Guides the student through the development of the reflective paper
- Discusses how to integrate reflection with the collected evidence
- Reviews drafts of the reflection paper
- Meets regularly with the student to ask probing questions, offer guidance, and assess progress at various steps in the process

Both the dean of the honors college and the curriculum coordinator are available to answer any questions or assist with any concerns at any point during the semester.

THE PORTFOLIO INTERVIEWS

At early meetings in the process with the student, the mentor, the curriculum coordinator, the academic advisor, the dean, and the review committee, we define the project clearly to both faculty and student, including criteria for evaluation. We set high expectations for 1) depth and freshness of reflection, 2) integration of reflection and artifacts, and 3) quality of writing style. We make sample portfolios available at this meeting; since each one is unique, the opportunity to survey the range of personal and creative approaches to the project often emboldens students to think big and take more risks with their own portfolios.

In a final meeting with the student, we review a draft copy of the portfolio to make suggestions for improvement at an exit interview before a final grade is determined by the faculty mentor. After conferring with the advisor, the student may or may not act upon the suggestions. In earlier years, in the absence of the initial meeting, portfolios sometimes reached the interview stage with substantial problems, and major revisions were requested. With clearer expectations, the quality of the portfolios at the interview is much higher, and the experience is a positive one for both students and faculty.

THE VALUE OF THE PORTFOLIO

Students who complete our portfolio project tell us that they find the experience enriching. For many students, the opportunity to integrate their academic, professional, and personal experiences in a thoughtful manner provides them for the first time with a glimpse of their own human complexity. They begin to see how a variety of experiences, that perhaps look disconnected on the surface, work together to shape a human being. Such understanding then provides the students with a solid foundation from which to approach the decisions and choices they need to make as they move into the next phase of their lives. Several students have commented, during our exit interview, on the value of this realization and have suggested that we encourage more students to complete the portfolio project. One student even has told us that we should require the portfolio! In addition, some of our students in the professional programs have enjoyed the opportunity to stretch creative muscles they didn't even know they had as they experimented with how to organize their artifacts and how best to present their reflection paper.

Karen Hewlett, a dance major who graduated in spring 2001, shared with us her thoughts about the portfolio project:

> I found the portfolio project to be an invaluable experience for me in my senior year...because it allowed me to reflect on the subject matter I was studying throughout the past four years while simultaneously evaluating how my personal view changed. I was able to look at the projects and opinions I had my freshman year and track my

creative and personal growth to my very final projects my
senior year. . . . The portfolio is a wonderful example of
how it is not the product but the process that is important
in life. . . .

Darwin Prioleau, Karen's faculty mentor, found the experience so valuable that she wondered whether she could require a similar project for all of
her dance majors:

Karen Hewlett's work on her Honors Portfolio may be one
of the most important experiences she has had at Kent.
Often college seniors are so busy looking forward to what
will happen after graduation that they fail to see the
importance of their four-year journey towards graduation.
Karen was able to take the time to reflect and learn from
her past experiences. I was astounded at how well she was
able to connect her past experiences and her present situation to her future aspirations.

Without exception, the faculty mentors have been impressed with the
nature and results of the portfolio project. They enjoy working closely with
individual students and find rewarding the opportunity to facilitate the personal development of students who have already proven themselves academically.

Persuasion, Politics, Pragmatics, and the Student Portfolio Movement

David G. Brown and H. David Womack
Wake Forest University

How does one cause all 4,000 Wake Forest University undergraduates to create and maintain a student portfolio? For us, the ideal is yet to be achieved. Still, herein we describe our highly successful pilot program and outline alternative strategies for spreading the portfolio practice throughout the entire student body.

SAMPLE PORTFOLIOS

Our student portfolios are all built from a common template. The top page is shown below. Under the top page are nested specific pages (e.g., résumé and aspirations).

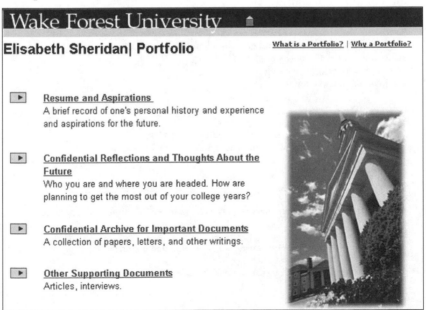

Publicly accessible areas are "resume and aspirations" and "other supporting documents." Materials not intended for open viewing are kept in a confidential area. The "confidential archive" and "support documents" areas warehouse digital materials. They may be viewed as the "digital bookshelves of a private library." The "resume and aspirations" and "reflections and thoughts" areas contain documents specifically authored for portfolio purposes. They often draw upon materials in the private library.

Samples of parts of actual portfolios constructed by different Wake Forest freshmen students show how these four areas are being used. Instructions for completing the résumé section are shown here:

Wake Forest University 🏛

Resume and Aspirations-

You should anticipate your desire to give this address to WF organizations who wish a biographical sketch for their records, potential summer and after-college employers, potential graduate school admission committees, and others. At this site most will want to include a picture, addresses (home, school, email, phones), honors and awards, major high school activities, college activities, volunteer activities, jobs, college major, career intentions.

Below is a sample résumé, without the picture and contact information that would compromise confidentiality.

Education:
- High-school diploma from Charlotte Catholic High School in Charlotte, NC.
- Graduated in top 15% of senior class.
- Member of Spanish Honor Society.
- Member of National Honor Society.

Extracurricular Activities:
- 15 years of ballet training.
- Member of Charlotte City Ballet Company from ages 13-18.
- Member of Charlotte Catholic High School dance team for three years.
- Member of SADD club.
- Member of Voices for Life.

Employment:
- Worked two consecutive summers (00, 01) as a lifeguard for Carmel Country Club.

Currently:
- A freshman at Wake Forest University with an undecided major.
- Member of the Wake Forest Dance Team
- Involved in various community service activities.

In the area on "confidential reflections and thoughts about the future," students are encouraged to write on three topics: career, family, and activities.

Wake Forest University

Thoughts about the Future

Career: After graduating Wake Forest University with a degree in Chemistry, or Business, I plan on going to graduate school to get an MBA. My goal is to work in the business side of Chemistry. Whether it be a pharmaceutical company, or a chemical plant, I plan to work in a field that I am interested in. If I am able to get a Chemistry degree and an MBA, I will be able to utilize my knowledge in chemistry to help sell my product.

Family: With the tragic events that have happened recently at the World Trade Center and Pentagon, I just hope that my close friends and family remain healthy. I have had such great luck in the past; I just hope that it continues. After I graduate and get settled down, raising a family would be next goal.

Activities: I have played baseball my entire life, and I presently am on the club baseball team. Continuing to play summer baseball in adult leagues and at school is my major physical goal. In the future, I plan on improving my guitar playing. In the next four years, I would like to get a group of friends together and play before an audience, possibly in a coffee house. I would also like to work in the area of community service, possibly helping aid the victims of the World Trade Center disaster.

The following is the index page from the "confidential archive for important documents."

Wake Forest University

Documents

This is my <u>Merit Scholarship Essay</u>

This is my <u>Women In Sports Essay</u>

This is my <u>First French Composition</u>

This is my <u>Kreamer Street Speach</u>

This is my <u>First Philosophy Essay</u>

This is my <u>Opportunity Cost Essay</u>

This is my <u>Scarcity Essay</u>

This is my <u>PowerPoint Presentation</u>

Although the framework is identical, all portfolios reflect the personalities of their authors. Variation is substantial. Frequent updating and revising is encouraged.

DEVELOPMENT STRATEGY

Few freshmen possess the computer skills necessary to design a web page that will not embarrass them ten years (or even ten months) later. Few recognize the dangers of disappearing electronic data, the power of lifetime planning, or the future value of a well-documented résumé. Therefore, if we were to successfully lure freshmen into the venture, it would be important to keep as low as possible the time and money costs of creating and maintaining a portfolio. The Wake Forest Portfolio Project proceeded under the following premises:

1) Students should be able to create their person portfolio in two hours or less.

2) The existence of the portfolio should not depend upon a continuing relationship between the student and Wake Forest University (e.g., the student should continue to have access to his or her portfolio even after graduation).

3) Materials within the portfolio should be able to be mixed and matched for future purposes not envisioned when data were first entered.

4) Self-management, without dependence upon computer professionals, should be possible.

5) Every portfolio should have both publicly accessible and totally confidential areas.

The goal of low cost (especially minimizing effort) was pursued by using familiar Internet browsers, encouraging students to plug in materials already created for other purposes, and having all students work from a common, professionally designed template. Platform independence and self-management were achieved periodically by burning portfolio files to students' own CDs.

UNDERSTANDING THE IMPORTANCE OF PORTFOLIOS

If students were voluntarily to create and maintain their portfolios, it was essential that they understand why. Three reasons were stressed.

To Market Yourself

Throughout life you will be competing for opportunities. While in college, they may be scholarships, memberships in honorary societies, internships, and positions in the most desirable study abroad programs. After college, the competition may be for graduate schools, professional placements, jobs, political office, awards, and honors. You will be advantaged by an accessible statement of who you are and what you have accomplished.

To Preserve Data

In our bygone paper world, unless you made a very conscious decision to keep your textbooks and term papers, copies remained available. In the information age, when papers (and some textbooks) are electronic, term papers may be lost when you upgrade computers. Textbooks may become inaccessible when you lose privileged access to the publishers' sites. Changes in software programs may render unreadable old digital documents. Materials conveniently available at a course web site will almost certainly not remain available after graduation. One must prudently defend against such losses by downloading important documents to one's personal portfolio.

To Help Anticipate

Anticipation takes two forms. First, as a society we had best anticipate that, sometime in the future, databases will be centered on individuals, not the institutional-centering of today. Already we see this trend in custom-designed, personal web pages, in nightly reports on the status of one's investment portfolio, in screen savers that include local weather information. Second, one of the major indications of individual success is the practice of personal planning, of setting goals and designing strategies to meet them. Portfolios provide a means and a discipline for such goal setting. Electronic reflections can be updated efficiently. Archiving is effortless.

Even before there is an all-college commitment to the portfolio principle, many individual students can be led to portfolios because of the substantial advantages.

POLITICS AND LEVERAGE

In spite of the rational advantages of portfolios, far too few take the initiative on their own. If portfolio creation is to touch almost all students, specific incentive strategies are necessary.

First-Year Seminar

Students in our pilot had to complete a portfolio as a requirement in a course that all students must take. Although we have not yet done this at Wake Forest, at some colleges and universities it would be fully feasible to mandate the development of a personal portfolio as a course requirement.

Placement Office

Offices that are outplacing graduates could insist upon résumés when students first register for the placement services. Short of requiring, these same offices could make registrants aware of the importance and power of easily accessible electronic résumés.

Information Technology

Wake Forest provides all students and faculty with a standard laptop computer. All computers contain a basic software package that could also include the portfolio template and a link to it from the homepage. In some colleges, information technology (IT) might even be able to require the completion of the template as a condition for receiving IT help.

Student Affairs and Student Government

By requiring the submission of portfolios of all applicants for, say, residence hall counsellorships or student government committees, portfolio development could be spread throughout the campus very quickly and with minimal costs.

Individual Departments

Short of an all-university mandate, individual academic departments might require the development of portfolios of their majors. Athletic departments might ask for portfolios from each intercollegiate athlete.

By suggesting these five very different agencies within the institution, we hope to imply that the leadership for a portfolio program can come from almost anywhere in the university, and certainly any collaborations would help spread portfolios rapidly!

CONCLUSION

As artists and architects have known for centuries, portfolios are important and helpful. By encouraging many different agencies throughout the university to consider requiring portfolios, by stressing the values of portfolios to individual students, and by keeping to a minimum the effort and costs of portfolio development, students can leave the institution with important intellectual, reflective, and practical skills grounded in the learning portfolio.

Demonstrating Mastery Through an Honors Portfolio

Earl B. Brown, Jr.
Radford University

Early in my tenure as honors director at Radford University, I realized that having students jump through additional hoops to demonstrate that they were honors material would be like developing honors courses that were quantitatively different rather than qualitatively different. What I believe distinguishes an honors student from other students is not the ability to do additional work, to jump through additional hoops, but rather the ability to do qualitatively significant work. But what is the best measure of such qualitative work? I discovered that the portfolio was a compelling tool for demonstrating honors learning.

DEFINING HONORS LEARNING

Let me briefly discuss my philosophical approach to honors as it underlies the development of the portfolio as part of honors graduation requirements. Requiring students enrolled in honors courses to do additional work does not demonstrate ability so much as motivation, drive, and determination. All of these traits are important, and no honors student should be without them. But what I really wanted from an honors student was perception, insight, and thoughtfulness. I wanted the student to think long and hard about issues raised in class, to explore these issues in greater depth both inside and outside the classroom. For this to happen, honors courses needed to assign less work not more, less breadth and coverage but more depth. Students should come out of an honors course with greater insight, although they may not have covered as much material as students enrolled in nonhonors sections of the same course. As I told many a prospective honors instructor, any instructor can assign lots of work. That is not what defines an honors class. Rather than the amount of work assigned, the depth of exploration is what distinguishes honors from nonhonors. Most of all, the active approach to learning places significant responsibility for learning on the students' shoulders, a key to distinguishing honors work.

If this is the philosophical approach I used to determine what made a course honors, I also needed to develop a similar approach to determine honors graduation requirements. I reviewed honors graduation requirements at many comparable institutions, and what I discovered came as no surprise. For students to graduate from an honors program, they needed to complete a certain number of hours in honors work, approximately 20% of their course work, and they needed to compile a certain grade point average, usually at least a 3.5 out of 4.0. All they needed to do was jump through hoops. The sole determining graduation factor was quantitative: take so many hours in honors and compile a certain grade point average. Given grade inflation, I discovered that many students could attain these quantitative requirements without truly understanding or learning much of anything or demonstrating the ability to become thoughtful, perceptive, and independent thinkers. (This is part of the reason for state-mandated assessment and for the need to find other means of assessing students' abilities and knowledge beyond grades. But that is a different chapter.)

IDENTIFYING HONORS OBJECTIVES

I knew then, just as I believe now, that I needed to urge the Honors Council to create objectives for the Honors Program. All students who graduated from the Honors Program would have to demonstrate that they had met the objectives. I reminded the council that in developing objectives, they needed to focus on what skills, abilities, and knowledge they expected students who graduated from honors to have. They need not concern themselves with the probability that nonhonors students might have developed the same skills and abilities and demonstrated similar knowledge:

Radford University Honors Program Objectives

- Effective written communication skills (including ability to use research)

- Effective oral communication skills

- The ability to analyze and synthesize a broad range of material

- The ability to formulate a problem, develop a plan of action, and prove or disprove a hypothesis or to create and produce an original work or do research

- The ability to take greater responsibility for one's own learning (demonstrate curiosity, motivation, risk-taking characteristics, and the ability to bring to bear logic and knowledge on the issue being discussed)

We might expect all students who graduate from a college or university to have such skills and abilities. Also, notice that all of the objectives are skills-based. The Honors Council believed that it is the application of knowledge that is important, not the knowledge itself.

Now that the program had objectives in place, it was time to review and reconstruct our approach to honors courses to ensure that enrolled students would have the opportunity to develop the skills and abilities. Thus, once Honors Program objectives were developed, everything else logically followed. In revising the honors course proposal form, the council offered the following advice to prospective instructors: "To help you think about your course objectives, we have listed below the Honors Program objectives which all Highlander Scholars must meet by the end of their third year." The council also provided a detailed discussion of methodology and means to incorporate each of the objectives into the course.

PORTFOLIO ASSESSMENT OF HONORS

The Honors Council then needed to decide what sort of assessment measure would be most effective in determining whether honors students had met Honors Program objectives. The council decided that a portfolio would be the most effective measure for several reasons. Most importantly, the portfolio allowed us to determine the nature and scope of the assessment measure. But beyond that, it provided students the opportunity to shape their own responses to the assessment. Students could choose any items they wanted from their years at Radford University or other institutions of higher learning. In this way, part of the assessment became the students' demonstration of the aptness of their selections in meeting the objectives, the reason why we placed such emphasis on the cover argument, in which we expected students to argue the merits of their selections. But the selling point for us was the reflective nature of the assignment. Giving students the opportunity to review their work over three years revealed their growth and change. They could see who they had become and the distance they had traveled to get there. The portfolio would also reveal implicitly, if not explicitly, their change in attitudes, a self-examination of affective behavior.

Now, it was time to implement the Honors Portfolio as a graduation requirement from Radford's Honors Program. Graduating from honors would no longer be determined only by quantitative measures. Students wishing to graduate would have to demonstrate quality as well. As I stated earlier, the fact that other students at Radford might develop similar skills and abilities was not an issue. What was at issue is that students outside the program would not have to demonstrate formally that they had such abilities in order to graduate from the university. The required process of reflection, demonstration of program objectives, and assessment of skills in a learning portfolio is what distinguishes Radford's Honors Program graduates.

The Honors Council decided that the portfolio would be due at the end of the junior year so that students would have an opportunity to resubmit if necessary. After two years, the council made the writing requirement (Objective A) due at the end of the sophomore year because so many of our students needed additional help with their writing. To guide students in creating a portfolio, I developed a set of instructions, reprinted below from the *RU Student Handbook.*

- All students graduating from the Honors Program will select samples from all honors and non-honors work completed in order to build a portfolio to demonstrate that the student has met the Honors Program Objectives. This portfolio will consist of a minimum of three to a maximum of six pieces of work that span the student's career at Radford University, at least one of which must be a written work involving research. The Honors Council requests that students submit both original with instructor comments as well as revisions where warranted for all written work submitted.

- This portfolio need not consist entirely of written work, but may include video or audiotapes, creative efforts (sculpture, paintings, designs, musical scores, dance choreographies, computer programs, to name but a few), and any other work the student believes demonstrates the Honors Program Objectives.

- The portfolio must also include a written discussion of why each piece is included as well as a statement explaining how other Honors Program Objectives have been or will be met, if the Objectives cannot be presented in a more tangible form.

- The Proposal Committee of the Honors Council will review students' submissions to determine if they have fulfilled Honors Program Objectives. If, upon review, a student does not fulfill all of these objectives, the student will have an opportunity to satisfy these objectives. If a student fails to meet objectives, that student will not be allowed to graduate from the Honors Program. Any decision made by the Proposal Committee may be appealed to the Honors Council within two weeks of the Committee's final decision.

In conversations with first-year students, I encouraged them to keep all of their work for possible inclusion in their portfolio. In conversations with third-year students, I explained that the key to the portfolio was their cover letter. In that letter they would need to justify the material that they included and how that material demonstrated the particular objective. I reminded them that the material selected did not have to come from honors courses nor did all of it have to be in written format. I also told students that when they graduated from honors, I would write a letter to be included with their transcript detailing what they had done to fulfill Honors Program requirements, especially noting that they had demonstrated competency in the skills and abilities that compose the Honors Program Objectives.

I advised the Proposal Committee of the Honors Council that its review of Honors Portfolios should focus on the cover letter as an argument. They were also reviewing portfolios to determine competency. If the student demonstrated competency, that student would have met the portfolio requirement of the Honors Program.

POSITIVE RESULTS OF HONORS PORTFOLIOS

The results of portfolio assessment were both gratifying and surprising. The committee approved approximately 95% of the portfolios submitted. Those that were not approved usually had difficulty with the writing objective, which is why the council decided to have that objective due earlier. As

I was a member of that committee (as were several students), I can vouch for the seriousness with which the committee reviewed the portfolios. The students were, in fact, the sternest taskmasters, as they wanted their honors degree to have significant meaning.

I was also gratified at the effect of the transcript insertion on graduate school acceptances and employment. Many of the students told me personally that the transcript insertion detailing their honors work and their competency in certain skills made the difference in their acceptance or their employment. All students told me that they did not view the creation of the portfolio as a chore, another hurdle to jump over, but as an opportunity to reflect on their career at Radford University. They were uniformly surprised at the quality of their work in the freshmen year: "How could I have written that?" "How could I have been so naïve as to believe that?" They were pleased at their development during their years at Radford, and in conversations with each other and with potential honors students, they said that the Honors Portfolio was the highlight of their career in honors and that it was the primary reason for students to give serious consideration to joining the Honors Program.

Creation of an Honors Portfolio as a requirement for graduation has proven to be effective for several reasons. It has made honors not just another quantitative exercise. Graduating from the Honors Program is not like graduating *cum laude*—it is not just a matter of completing so many hours and compiling a certain grade point average. Students who graduate from Radford's Honors Program do meet minimum criteria for honors hours completed and a grade point average, but they also must demonstrate that they have met specific competencies. Honors graduation is quantitative, to be sure, but more importantly it is qualitative, providing an opportunity for students to reflect on their education. Looking at past work reminds them of what they had been like and how far they have come. This reflective aspect of creating a portfolio is to me the most important educational component of the task.

And finally, honors directors and other educators are always looking for ways to assess change in affective attitudes. Did the Honors Program develop the student's sense of responsibility? Change a student's attitudes toward race or sexual orientation? Develop a student's sense of citizenship, of obligation to the community? Develop a student's ability to lead? The Honors Portfolio provides an excellent means to assess such affective change and to demonstrate mastery of honors learning.

Changing How Students Think About Writing: The Web-Based Learning Environment Project Portfolio

Jená A. Burges
Longwood College

Paradoxically, one of the biggest challenges in teaching freshman composition is that most capable students have done well in writing at the high school level. Given their successful track records, they rely heavily on strategies that have worked for them in the past. Some of these strategies, however, fail them when they approach the dizzying range of writing tasks in their college classes.

As they enter college, many students must move beyond their accustomed view of writing as a fairly simple mechanical process. Unfortunately, their confidence in the writing approach they already know can be a barrier to learning the new strategies they will need. In order to develop as writers at this new level, they must first see a need to "think different" about writing, in both of the ways implied by the intentionally ambiguous Apple Computer slogan. They must learn both to reframe their view of what writing is (to think different[ly] about writing) and to think explicitly about different kinds of writing (to think "different," as in "think snow" or "think pink"). Crafting a learning portfolio can provide both the stimulus for such shifts in thinking and a record of how the shifts occur.

Technology, Writing, Teaching, and Learning

The reference to a computer slogan is appropriate because the portfolio project described here was undertaken in the first year of a laptop computer initiative. The new hardware was suddenly everywhere; its social, political, and educational implications demanded the critical thinking, analysis, reading, and writing that are central to freshman composition courses. Otherwise, we were in danger of encouraging students to be unquestioning, unreflective consumers of technology rather than active agents in analyzing what its role in their lives should be. It seemed particularly appropriate to probe such complexities in the context of a freshman composition class because opportunities to investigate how literacy itself was being reshaped by technology would motivate students to think in newly critical ways about their own writing.

Another important, if entirely unplanned, factor also helped in moving the students toward reframing their views of writing: When the semester began, we discovered that everyone in the class intended to become teachers. They began to make connections among technology, teaching, learning, and writing when they read an article by Kay (1997), reprinted in our reader:

> The physicist Murray Gell-Mann has remarked that education in the 20th century is like being taken to the world's greatest restaurant and being fed the menu. He meant that representations of ideas have replaced the ideas themselves; students are taught superficially about great discoveries instead of being helped to learn deeply for themselves. (p. 151)

Kay goes on to describe how technology has the potential for structuring learning in new ways, allowing children to experience a range of data and documents from multiple perspectives in order to learn deeply for themselves. As we discussed the implications of such ideas, the connections began to emerge. I began to realize that not only was this experience of deep learning exactly what my students needed so that they could learn a new view of writing, but it was also exactly what I was trying to teach them about what well-crafted texts do for readers. How could I set up a learning experience that would make the most of the parallels they were beginning to see between effective teaching and effective writing?

The answer started with a suggestion from editors Hawisher and Selfe (1997) for responding to the Kay article with a proposal for a web site. The idea grew into the Web-Based Learning Environment Project Portfolio, a learning portfolio venture that pushed my students to learn deeply for themselves that both teaching and writing are complex problem solving processes aimed at changing their audiences. The connection became both a guide for the process and a focus for the products of the portfolio.

FEEDING THEM FOOD INSTEAD OF MENUS

Beginning in the third week of the semester, the portfolio presented the future teachers with the educational problems of identifying a specific group of learners needing a particular skill or knowledge base, developing a web-based resource that would immerse those learners in complex learning processes, and persuading college authorities that their web-based learning environment deserved space on the campus server. This was a complicated problem, and composition textbook prescriptions would not be much help. Instead, students began by selecting a target audience, thinking about what they were like and how they were different from other readers who had to be addressed. They defined their problem and produced five documents aimed at solving it, with an introduction as the central reflective element of the portfolio.

In grappling with the problem, my students were themselves immersed in complex learning processes. They identified and analyzed two distinct audiences to whom they had to write differently and for different purposes. They figured out the knowledge, limitations, and concerns of their readers. They designed documents and organizational arrangements to meet the needs of those different readers and thus to accomplish their goals as writers. They talked about how to understand their readers better and how to make the many decisions involved in moving the readers along. And as they planned how they wanted their target audiences to experience the components of the web-based learning environments, they learned deeply for themselves about the complexity of both teaching and writing. When they wrote the introduction section of their portfolios, they synthesized and reflected on what they had learned, rounding out the complete learning portfolio.

LEARNING ABOUT AUDIENCE

Students in the class chose an amazing range of learner groups to address and learning goals to achieve with their web-based learning environments. Choosing a target audience for their learning environment and the materials reflected in their portfolios was important, but having to think about why they were making their choices was more challenging for students. Melissa specifically chose children in grades K–5 for her audience, hoping that "by exposing them early to alternative methods of learning and opposing viewpoints... they will develop the ability to think for themselves and consult several sources before forming their opinions." In explaining that she did not choose to address her own peer group "because [she] felt that the existing resources available to them are sufficient and meet their needs," Dana demonstrated having learned a basic prerequisite for effective writing: Find a gap and fill it.

LEARNING ABOUT PROCESS

Research indicates that novice writers engage in knowledge-telling, simply writing down what they know about a topic as it occurs to them. Expert writers, on the other hand, frame their writing tasks as complex problems to be solved, and they create new knowledge in the process of making multiple decisions about what to write and how to write it (Scardamalia & Bereiter, 1987). When they enter college, even very bright students who conscientiously outline, draft, and revise (which usually means light editing) tend to have a novice's oversimplified view of the writing process as a straightforward series of operations, rather than a rather untidy problem solving process that is complicated and difficult to manage.

The nature of the portfolio project prevented students from taking a simple, linear approach, and students became very aware of how their processes changed as a result. Aimee wrote that "everything had to be done over and over again, until I got close to what I wanted it to be." Melissa described how useful it was to get feedback from her classmates during the process of producing each type of text because it made her "think in a broader sense instead of just the one track mind I tend to develop as I try so hard to focus on my project's purpose." They learned that improvement was always possible, even for a good text. As they moved toward the problem solving orientation of expert writers, they became aware that they were creating new knowledge as they made writing decisions.

LEARNING ABOUT TEXTS

Producing a portfolio consisting of a variety of text types that were related yet distinct from one another gave the students a much deeper awareness of text characteristics and how they related to the intended audiences, purposes, and formats. The importance of graphic appearance, whether a text was a traditional research paper format or an interactive web page, was foundational, as Dana pointed out: "Even though the text was important, the arrangement of the text was crucial . . . It seemed that the visual elements were emphasized as much as the textual elements were." More basic elements of written texts were also foregrounded for the students, as Robert pointed out when he wrote that preparing his portfolio "further extended my understanding of organization, a very important factor in writing. ..."

LEARNING ABOUT LEARNING

Learning, like writing, requires reflection. It is neither mechanical nor straightforward. A writing task represents a problem to be solved, requiring analysis and reflection throughout the process. What must I do to solve this problem? Who are the readers? What do they need to know? What am I missing? How is this like something I've done before, and how is it different?

In pulling the portfolio together, students were confronted at every turn with situations that required just such reflection. In the process, they grappled with the connections among technology, teaching, learning, and writing. Did such reflection in their portfolios help them to identify and understand the connections? I'll let Dana answer that one:

> This project was simply the embodiment of the rhetorical devices that we were supposed to have a greater understanding of at the end of this course. ... [The portfolio was] very different from projects I have completed in the past, in that this one forced me to actually create—we learned about learning itself.

REFERENCES

Hawisher, G. E., & Selfe, C. L. (Eds.). (1997). *Literacy, technology, and society: Confronting the issues.* Upper Saddle River, NJ: Prentice-Hall.

Kay, A. C. (1997). Computers, networks and education. In G. E. Hawisher & C. L. Selfe (Eds.), *Literacy, technology, and society: Confronting the issues* (pp. 150–158). Upper Saddle River, NJ: Prentice-Hall. (Original work published 1991)

Scardamalia, M., & Bereiter, C. (1987). Knowledge telling and knowledge transforming in written composition. In S. Rosenberg (Ed.), *Advances in applied psycholinguistics* (Vol. 2, pp. 142–175). New York, NY: Cambridge University Press.

Portfolios Within an Honors Program: The Honors Preparation Year and Beyond

Candee C. Chambers
Mercyhurst College

Portfolios play a prominent role in the Mercyhurst College Honors Program, a sophomore- through senior-year program that students must apply to join in the spring of the freshman year. The selection process is based primarily upon a portfolio that the students create in the first two-thirds of their first year on campus. Once admitted to the program, students submit yearly updates.

The portfolios and the updates include items related to competency assessment, career preparation, and reflective process documents. In the four years that students spend creating and updating their portfolios, they are encouraged to think about both content and reflective learning. The portfolios are also used as a vehicle to initiate dialogue for student growth.

PORTFOLIOS IN THE HONORS PREPARATION YEAR

Incoming freshmen are admitted to a trial program that we call the Honors Preparation Year (HPY). In this trial period, HPY students try out the program's classes and activities, and the program gets to try them out at the same time. At the end of this trial period (the spring of their first year), they submit a portfolio to a faculty selection committee. The purpose of the HPY is to allow students to sample our program before formally committing to becoming a member and to prepare them for the sophomore-through senior-year portion of the program. An integral part of the process is a portfolio that each student creates during the first two-thirds of the first year.

Portfolios for Assessment

The Honors Program office reviews portfolios prior to submitting them to the selection committee. Students with egregious deficiencies in their portfolios are contacted immediately. Their portfolios are not forwarded to the selection committee unless the deficiencies are ones that can be corrected quickly. Portfolios reviewed for assessment purposes must include a college transcript, a form indicating meeting/event attendance, and letters of recommendation from faculty at the college. Also, the QPA must be close to the 3.0 requirement and an honors course must have been taken with a grade of C or better.

PORTFOLIOS FOR CAREER PREPARATION

The initial screening of portfolios allows us to initiate important dialogues with students. Most students in our program intend to pursue graduate educations. Students who turn in portfolios that are deficient in clearly outlined requirements and that we believe could be strengthened benefit from early dialogues regarding professionalism. We believe that we are giving our students a good head start in thinking about graduate school application requirements and optimal ways of describing one's accomplishments by initiating this dialogue at the end of the freshman year of college. Transcript analysis also leads to discussions concerning strategies for course selection.

The letter of application is the portfolio component that we find to be the most frequently used in terms of career preparation for the HPY portfolios. Students have the opportunity to attend a workshop on writing a letter of application prior to the submission of their portfolios; thus, they do not enter the process without initial guidance. However, many of the letters of application that students submit in their portfolios need some refining. Most college students go through this learning and revising process in their junior or senior years. We believe that by initiating the process earlier, we give our students an edge in the competitive arena of graduate programs, graduate stipends, internships, fellowships, or scholarships. Often, students are presented with such opportunities during the academic year, when they have other responsibilities that they may consider more pressing at that time. Students who have been through our portfolio process have a reviewed draft of an application letter ready for revision to suit the opportunity at hand. This mentored process is an important career preparation tool.

Portfolios for Reflection

Two components of the HPY portfolios are reflective in nature. First, the application letter requires students to reflect on their long-term career goals (at least the next four to ten years) as opposed merely to thinking about next year's courses in their major. Good application letters should also describe what students believe that they as scholars and as people bring to our Honors Program and to the intellectual/cultural community at the college. Many students have never been asked to undertake such an endeavor.

Second, the service-learning requirement of the HPY requires students to write a two-page service-learning reflection paper for the portfolio. Our service-learning office at the college emphasizes that the writing of the reflection paper is a vital capstone to the experience.

Portfolios and the Goals of the Honors Program

A few of the main goals of the program are described in this section. Keep in mind that the goals are reflected in the portfolio updates required of sophomores, juniors, and seniors:

- Creating classroom settings wherein exceptionally good students can utilize their intellectual and creative gifts to achieve academic distinction

- Encouraging our exceptional students to bring their talents for, and attitudes about, pursuing the academic life to the larger community, creating a richer and more vibrant Mercyhurst College

- Making service to other human beings an important and pervasive part of our exceptional students' lives

- Preparing our extraordinary students for lives in which research, publication and presentation of ideas, membership in professional communities, and leadership are defining characteristics

We seek to accomplish such goals through yearly requirements, and students must document the requirements in the form of yearly portfolio updates.

Portfolios in the Sophomore- Through Senior-Year Honors Program

Once students are in the Honors Program, they maintain annual updates to the portfolio that they initially submitted as part of their application to the program. For all three years, portfolios include the following items:

- Honors-certified event attendance/creation cards
- Two-page service reflection paper
- Current transcript
- Current résumé

In the junior year, they also submit a two-page form with details regarding their senior thesis. In the senior year, they submit their thesis with their portfolio update.

Portfolios for Assessment
As with the HPY portfolio, transcripts and honors-certified event attendance/creation cards allow us to assess each student's achievement of the program's minimum requirements.

Portfolios for Career Preparation
Just as the letter of application is an important career preparation component of the HPY portfolio, the résumé is an important career-oriented part of the portfolio update. Most sophomores find themselves preparing their first résumé to fulfill the portfolio requirement. Students typically seek out appropriate faculty or a specialized college office or department that aids students in résumé preparation. Once the initial résumé is created, we recommend keeping it on hand to modify as needed for any career opportunities that present themselves throughout the academic year. We teach students that being organized and planning ahead, not just in coursework, make it easier for busy professionals to be successful.

Portfolios for Reflection
As students revise their résumés in the junior and senior years, we often find that deep reflection has occurred as a result of the process. Several students have included a one-page reflection paper inspired by the changes that they have elected to make. We do not require this assignment as part of the portfolio update, but students generally feel that they have made such dramatic changes to their résumés that they wish to include an explanation. Such extra effort suggests that students use the revising requirement of the portfolio update not merely as a career development tool, but also as a time to reflect on their goals.

As with the HPY portfolio, students also write a two-page reflection paper based on their 15 hours of service learning. Some students elect to perform service learning at the same place every year. Other students, particularly those with less rewarding experiences, choose to seek out entirely different types of service-learning experiences. In either case, when looking at any one student's service-learning reflection papers for all four years, both student and faculty can see the changes that have taken place in the student's perspectives, goals, and values during the college career.

Finally, the portfolio updates encourage student reflection as they begin to look at how their portfolio and updates have changed from year to year. Often the types of events that they elect to attend change dramatically. Typically, they shift their involvement to be either more varied in topic (some dance performances, discussion groups, foreign films, science lectures) or more narrow in scope (nearly all events related to their majors).

CONCLUSION

The portfolios and updates that the students have created and maintained for four years as part of the Mercyhurst College Honors Program are effective learning tools in their creation alone. However, many students find that the portfolios are most useful during the senior year. Portfolios are available for students applying to graduate programs. They are helpful in recalling a comprehensive list of events that they have attended or created while on campus. By the senior year, the list is impressive. They also review their service reflection papers through the years. Many students find career-related service venues. Students may also request that the portfolios be loaned out to faculty members, who may find the portfolios helpful in providing well-organized and well-documented information for inclusion in letters of recommendation.

Seniors often also speak of simply enjoying a quiet moment reading their portfolios and reflecting upon the documentation of the years they have spent within our college community and in the Honors Program.

Learning Portfolios: A Powerful Tool for Enhancing Course Design

L. Dee Fink
University of Oklahoma

Every time teachers get ready to teach a course, they have to make a number of decisions about the nature of the instructional experience they are trying to create. This can be done casually and superficially, or it can be done thoroughly and systematically. For teachers who choose the latter approach, learning portfolios have enormous value.

In this chapter, I present a brief overview of a model of integrative course design that is elaborated more fully in Fink (2003), and I use the model to reveal the reasons why learning portfolios have such important potential value.

A MODEL OF INTEGRATIVE COURSE DESIGN

The model for designing learning experiences includes the same primary components as others. What is distinctive about the model is that it assembles those components in a way that is simple and yet unpacks to reveal the complexity of actual teaching. It also makes clear the interactions among the components.

The basic model itself is shown in Figure 1. The rectangular box refers to information that needs to be collected and analyzed; the three circles refer to decisions that need to be made. The model suggests five key steps in the design process.

Step 1: Situational Factors
The first step is for the teacher to collect information about a number of situational factors and then analyze the information to determine how it may

Figure 1

A Model of Integrative Course Design

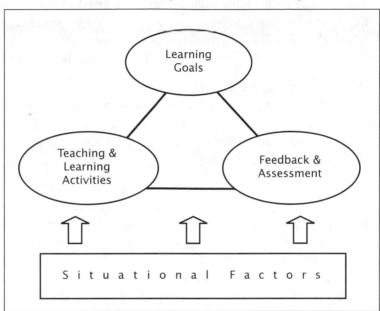

affect the three primary decisions. Five general kinds of factors that a teacher should consider follow:

- **Specific context:** class size, level of the course, time structure

- **General context:** curriculum, professional licensing, delivery (live, online, combination)

- **Nature of the subject:** convergent or divergent, stable or in flux, physical skills

- **Student characteristics:** prior knowledge, attitudes, personal situation, reason(s) for enrolling

- **Teacher characteristics:** level of development, experience teaching the course, centrality of course to core expertise.

Step 2: Learning Goals

The next step is to decide what the teacher would like for students to glean from a course. Goals need to be more than clear; they need to focus on significant kinds of higher-level learning.

Step 3: Feedback and Assessment

After deciding what the desired kinds of learning are, the teacher can work on the related question of what students have to do to convince the teacher that they have achieved the learning goals. Similarly, what would allow students themselves to know whether they are achieving the learning goals? Answers to such questions constitute feedback and assessment procedures.

Step 4: Teaching/Learning Activities

A key part of the design process concerns what the teacher and students will do during the course to realize the learning goals. If the course is going to achieve higher-level learning goals, activities must reflect the principles of active learning and reflective dialogue.

Step 5: Integration

The final step in this part of the process is making sure that the learning goals, the feedback and assessment procedures, and the teaching/learning activities are well integrated. That is, all three components need to reflect and support each other.

Again, the preceding comments are only a brief glimpse at the key steps in the model of integrative course design detailed in Fink (2003). To understand the value of learning portfolios, we also need to unpack the two components that directly address what actually happens in the course: the teaching/learning activities and the feedback and assessment procedures. And this means taking a closer look at the concepts of active learning and educative assessment.

ACTIVE LEARNING

The two activities that are most widely used at the present time in higher education, lecturing and reading assignments, fulfill one important function in learning: they provide information and ideas. But powerful learning requires more, and such recognition is what has prompted increased interest in active learning in higher education. Bonwell and Eison (1991) define active learning as "involving students in doing things and thinking about what they are doing" (p. *iii*).

The combined functions of both passive and active learning are shown in Figure 2. The diagram suggests that to have a powerful learning experience, students need all three sets of learning activities. They need to have 1) a good source of information and ideas, 2) some kind of doing or observing experience, and 3) opportunities to engage in reflective dialogue with themselves or with others. Integration among these three forms of learning is also important. The doing activities need to relate to the content; the reflection needs to be about the content and the doing or observing experiences.

FIGURE 2

A Model of Active Learning

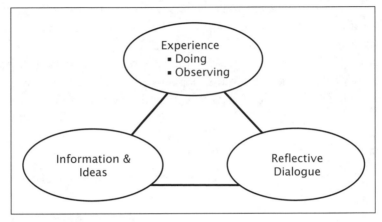

EDUCATIVE ASSESSMENT

Some teachers take a minimalist approach to feedback and assessment: "Two mid-terms and a final, and we're out of here." That suffices to give the teacher a basis for assigning a course grade to students, but it does little or nothing to help the learning process itself. Feedback and assessment activities that do enhance the learning process are called educative assessment (Wiggins, 1998).

In order to support the learning process, such assessment procedures need to have clear criteria and standards and need to be forward looking, that is, anticipating students' potential future use of their knowledge in situations where the knowledge acquires meaning. Students also need to have opportunities for self-assessment, and teachers' assessment feedback needs to be Frequent, Immediate, Discriminating, and delivered Lovingly. When this is done, the teacher has provided "FIDeLity" feedback, a concept I elaborate elsewhere (Fink, 2003). When the teacher includes all four of these basic components, the students will have the kind of feedback and assessment which truly aids the learning process itself.

THE EDUCATIONAL VALUE OF LEARNING PORTFOLIOS

Now we have a basis for understanding the special educational value of learning portfolios. The reason portfolio development has such significance is that it creates a powerful link between good teaching/learning activities and good feedback and assessment procedures. As illustrated in Figure 3, learning portfolios simultaneously provide students with an opportunity to engage in reflective dialogue and self-assessment. Students have to assess the quality of their own learning and then reflect on what they have learned, the significance of what they have learned, and how they have learned. As a result of such linkages, the assessment drives good learning and the learning drives good assessment. When this happens, the teacher has succeeded in designing a course in which the goals of assessment-as-learning have real meaning.

FIGURE 3

The Integrative Relationship of Learning Portfolios

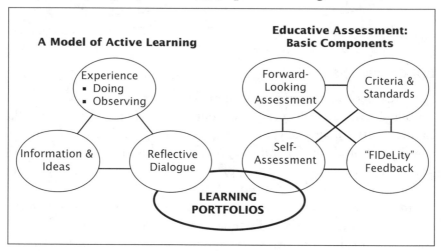

INCREASING STUDENTS' SELF-AWARENESS AS LEARNERS

Having students create a learning portfolio at the end of a course can be a valuable learning experience. People who put together any kind of portfolio generally report that doing so not only creates a product that summarizes their learning but also increases the quantity and quality of the learning. But the process of learning is even more powerful when the teacher gives students opportunities throughout the course to engage in reflective dialogue and self-assessment.

Two mechanisms for doing so during the course are one-minute papers and periodic reflective writing in a course journal. At the end of a class session or in the final class of the week, the teacher might ask students to reflect and write for one minute on several questions:

- How might you use what you have learned thus far in the course (or after the course is over)?

- What idea did you find most interesting or exciting? Which most puzzling?

- How did you learn? What was most helpful to your learning? What was not helpful?

- What other ways might you have tried to learn what you needed to learn?

When students repeatedly engage in such reflective dialogue and thereby assess the quality of their learning, they gradually become more self-aware of themselves as learners. This is important because students, like everyone else, can get in the habit of going through the motions of taking lecture notes, doing their homework, and taking exams—all rather thoughtlessly. When this happens, they do not really know what they have learned and their learning can easily have a short life before forgetting starts to set in. On the other hand, if they are prompted to reflect and self-assess regularly in a course, they begin to become more mindful learners and thereby become more aware of what they are learning, how they are learning, and the value of their learning. This can be extremely important in promoting a deep approach to learning.

BECOMING SELF-DIRECTING LEARNERS

Once students become more fully aware of themselves as learners, they are in a good position to start the process of controlling and shaping other learning activities in their lives. They can look at the personal, social, and work life they would like to have and identify what they need to learn to achieve that kind of life. Once they have identified what they need and want to learn, they can work on identifying how they would learn. Such learning might involve, for instance, reading a book, observing an action, trying something new to see how it works, talking to a mentor, interviewing an expert, or taking a course. Looking at what they need and want to learn, students can combine that information with their own newly acquired understanding of how they learn best and formulate an effective learning strategy.

Once students have learned how to formulate their own learning agendas in life and effective learning strategies for pursuing those agendas, they have, in essence, become effective, self-directing learners.

THE PHYSICAL AND PSYCHOLOGICAL VALUE OF REFLECTION

Many writers recognize the significance of periodically engaging in reflection, an activity strongly promoted by learning portfolios. Leamnson (2000) and others who have explored the educational implications of brain research have stressed the importance of reflection in creating the strong and stable neural pathways necessary for durable learning. Engaging in doing experiences—active learning—stimulates emotions, and that is important. But reflection then links experience and emotions to the neural pathways of the brain where information and ideas are stored and can be recalled. Hence, reflection is crucial in creating learning that lasts.

Other writers have addressed the psychological value of reflection. Palmer (2000) has noted the significance of what he calls "inner work" (p. 91) and reflection for people in leadership positions, a situation in which many college graduates will find themselves. Reflection, he feels, is necessary for the authentic self-understanding that must precede working effectively with others to build strong community.

Again, teachers who incorporate learning portfolios into the design of their courses offer students multiple opportunities to engage in the kind of introspection and reflection that has major educational and developmental value.

CONCLUSION

Learning portfolios are a powerful educational tool whose time has come. The scholarship of teaching has recognized the importance of active learning, educative assessment, and integrative course design. Learning portfolios are an effective means of accomplishing and integrating all three aspects of best practice in college teaching.

If teachers can learn how to use learning portfolios in their individual courses, and if departmental curriculum committees can introduce learning portfolios into multiple course experiences, our students will leave college much better prepared to engage in important life activities. They will have extensive experience in knowing 1) how to reflect meaningfully on their own learning, 2) how to assess the quality and value of their learning and their performance in multiple areas of life, and 3) how to know the value of, and have the skills for, being effective self-directing learners the rest of their lives. What wonderful additions to higher education that would be!

REFERENCES

Bonwell, C. C., & Eison, J. A. (1991). *Active learning: Creating excitement in the classroom* (ASHE-ERIC Higher Education Report No. 1). Washington, DC: George Washington University.

Fink, L. D. (2003). *Creating significant learning experiences in college classrooms: An integrated approach to designing college courses.* San Francisco, CA: Jossey-Bass.

Leamnson, R. (2000). Learning as biological brain change. *Change, 32* (6), 34–40.

Palmer, P. J. (2000). *Let your life speak: Listening for the voice of vocation.* San Francisco, CA: Jossey-Bass.

Wiggins, G. (1998). *Educative assessment: Designing assessments to inform and improve student performance.* San Francisco, CA: Jossey-Bass.

Experiential Learning Portfolios in Professional Programs: A Canadian Perspective

Eileen Herteis
University of Saskatchewan

More and more, professional program areas are beginning to see that students need paid or volunteer experiential learning opportunities afforded by the workplace in order to apply the theoretical knowledge they have acquired in the classroom and to obtain the skills they need to succeed as professionals: problem solving, decision making, adaptability, teamwork, and organization. Internships, practicums, experiential learning programs, and professional practice experiences enrich the curriculum for students and help to forge important links between the university and professionals in the field; however, they bring their own challenges. Simply deciding to implement experiential learning opportunities is one thing; to construct them so that the learning flows seamlessly from classroom to workplace is another. There are questions of structure and assessment:

- What is the relationship between what goes on off-campus and on-campus?

- How can we be sure that these experiences promote student learning goals and teachers' objectives?

- How can we design internships or experiential learning opportunities to ensure that they represent the intersection of learning with experience, theory with practice?

- How can we assess students' learning when there is no set content, a wide diversity of activity, and not much opportunity to test the outcomes?

For three professional colleges at the University of Saskatchewan in Canada, the answer to such questions was experiential learning portfolios. The College of Agriculture, the division of dietetics in the College of Pharmacy and Nutrition, and the College of Education worked to develop guidelines for students that would help them to transform experience into learning through structured reflection and documentation, while at the same time providing faculty with robust standards of evaluation. These colleges took advantage of another development on campus, an investigation of Prior Learning Assessment and Recognition (PLAR), to develop principles for the documentation and assessment of experiential learning. PLAR is a systematic process to evaluate and give recognition to learning that takes place outside formal educational institutions. A basic premise of PLAR is that significant learning can and does take place outside the classroom. Most commonly, those who seek assessment of their prior learning for credit are people who have been working for a number of years. Portfolios are one of the ways that such experiential learning can be documented and assessed. Therefore, the principles of PLAR apply suitably to internships, practicums, or off-campus learning opportunities.

In 1997, the Saskatchewan government provided funding to the province's two universities to investigate implementation of PLAR. Over two years, ten pilot projects were created to examine how PLAR principles could be used to evaluate experiential learning for university credit. This chapter examines three of the projects, still ongoing at the University of Saskatchewan. (For more about PLAR, see http://www.extension.usask.ca/ExtensionDivision/resources/PLAR/home.html.)

All three of the colleges have used portfolios as the way to document the experiential learning that took place during the internship or work placement. Similarly, all three have found that the process of self-reflection and the examination and selection of materials which the portfolio prompts are crucial to linking learning with experience. Portfolios help students to translate experience into learning through reflection, analysis, and documentation (Hutchings & Wutzdorff, 1988).

As Wong (1999), principal investigator of the Saskatchewan Universities PLAR Project, says, "When learners analyze and document their prior learning, they are describing how they have acquired new knowledge or developed new skills through the transformation of personally meaningful experience" (p. 20). Portfolio assessment is particularly attractive in connecting activities in the classroom with the world beyond because it includes assessment of active learning and performance rather than the mere recall of facts. Indeed, experiential learning opportunities coupled with portfolio assessment may be a way to counteract what Nelson (2001) calls bulimic learning: students' tendency to stuff themselves with facts that they have not digested properly and that they have no intention of remembering past the regurgitation at the exam. According to Nelson, "no mental nourishment remains" (p. 10).

The success of portfolio programs, however, depends upon objectives established beforehand and the guidance and support students receive as they work and learn off-campus. In the following examples of practice from the University of Saskatchewan, we see how institutional support and student guidelines have created a climate for success in the development of experiential learning portfolios. All emphasize that learning happens as a result of the creative integration of reflection and experience. Each of these colleges has given careful consideration to setting the scene for reflection and reflective critique from peers, faculty, and workplace colleagues.

DOCUMENTING EXPERIENTIAL LEARNING IN THE COLLEGE OF AGRICULTURE

> "The purpose is to allow students to *recall* the past, *review* the present, and *reflect* on the past in order to plan for the future."
>
> *(College of Agriculture: Work Term Report Guidelines)*

Up to 60 students a year participate in the College of Agriculture's experiential education program (a four-month work term placement or internship program). At the end of each placement, students submit a work term report that closely approximates the experiential learning portfolio. In 1998, the college realized that there were opportunities to enhance the work term experience and outcomes for the students by instituting more rigorous guidelines for the report which emphasized reflection on what was learned during the work experience rather than simple chronological narration of what took place. A number of things had become clear:

1) There seemed to be no way of assessing the (academic) success of the work term.

2) Students focused on what they had done rather than what they had learned.

3) Students often failed to see that they could learn even from a negative experience.

4) The work term seemed to be isolated from the rest of the learning experience.

5) There was little chance for interaction between the university and the workplace.

There have been two important changes: the introduction of a form on formulating learning objectives and a set of report guidelines (see Part IV of this volume).

Students are urged to think consciously about their goals for the learning experience, setting objectives (both in the cognitive and affective domain) that help them both establish desired outcomes and identify unplanned results of the experience. Students obtain ownership of the experience by relating each objective to an evaluation of success. Furthermore, the objectives are divulged to the employer and to the college so that there is now a partnership linking the work placement to in-class learning. The following information is from the College of Agriculture's student guidelines on designing work term objectives:

The objective has four characteristics. It should be:

1) Focused directly on the job

2) Developed in conjunction with the employer

3) Representative of activities to be done during the work experience

4) Measurable

Agriculture students keep a journal or diary of their learning experiences during the work term, and they are urged to reflect both in and on action.

The clarity of the report guidelines and the emphasis on reflection help students to derive the maximum potential benefit from the experiential learning opportunity. The guidelines help build student morale by demonstrating how to turn perceived gaps into learning opportunities and to take stock of their success and growth.

In the three years since the new experiential learning program and new guidelines have been implemented, we have noted that students are more deliberate in trying to get the most out of their experiential learning opportunities so that they fulfill their objectives. Their reports are more than a leisurely ramble through "What I did on my work term." Students are less passive and more assertive in seeking learning opportunities. A corollary of this gain is that supervising employers are very happy with the students' performance and the collaborative approach to experiential learning in which they and the students are engaged.

The college hopes to fold the guiding principles for the work term report into guidelines for a career-readiness or exit portfolio that would build incrementally as the student pursues the degree program.

THE DIVISION OF DIETETICS
IN THE COLLEGE OF PHARMACY AND NUTRITION

As a result of 1995 program revisions, the division of dietetics in the College of Pharmacy and Nutrition made a number of curriculum changes. Two new professional practice courses were designed whereby third- and fourth-year dietetics students would learn through professional application and demonstrate their achievement of learning objectives through portfolios. The goal was to introduce more practice into the dietetics program not just by adding more examples, but by integrating practical, sustained, experiential learning. During the design process, we also realized that the new courses needed a different form of assessment.

Students are involved in this process from start to finish, in what the director of the program, Dr. Shawna Berenbaum, describes as a continuum of self-directed learning. In completing the two semester-long professional practice courses, students must fulfill a number of objectives: their own learning objectives, the objectives and assessment criteria of the college, and the objectives for the professional standards and required competencies of the Professional Dietitians of Canada.

Students create a reflective self-assessment of their background, interests, past experience, and skills, selecting a number of congruent experiential learning opportunities. Some of the opportunities are individual; others are group or pair work, mirroring the kinds of activities which a professional dietitian will perform.

After individual meetings with faculty, students are matched with appropriate projects based on their self-assessment and stated objectives. Students also create an action plan and set their own timelines. Before their practicum begins, they attend a portfolio workshop where they are introduced to the ten learning objectives they must fulfill in four competence areas:

1) Application of nutrition knowledge

2) Assessment, planning, implementation, and evaluation

3) Communication

4) Professionalism

Reflection and continuous supportive feedback during the practicum provide the basis for progress and the cycle of improved professional practice. During the projects, students keep a reflective journal of what they are learning and observing. From the supervising dietitian with whom they are cooperating, they acquire feedback on their performance and on their project's progress. The feedback and letters from their supervising dietitians go into their portfolios. Students also submit monthly progress reports during their professional practice course. The reports contain a description of achievements, how they are meeting their objectives, and reflection on learning and skills acquired.

Furthermore, three times during the course, students gather to discuss their projects, professional standards, and learning. From faculty and from one another, they receive feedback, suggestions, and ideas. One of these meetings mixes the fourth-year students with the third-year students so that they can learn from their peers, demonstrating that learning portfolio mentors can be both faculty and peers, a lesson emphasized in Part I of this volume. The college has set the climate for student involvement by asking volunteer students who have taken the course to correspond with faculty who revise the guidelines for the course every year.

The college faculty and the project supervisors are committed to this process of experiential learning. Although time-consuming, it is eminently rewarding.

The students like both the experiential learning opportunities and the portfolio process. Once submitted, the portfolios are graded pass or fail by committee, based on the student's fulfillment of the stated competence areas, goals, and learning objectives. Students are enormously proud of their portfolios as concrete manifestations of their learning achievements.

DOCUMENTING EXPERIENTIAL LEARNING
IN THE COLLEGE OF EDUCATION

Students in the final year of the bachelor of education program complete a major practicum, a 16-week internship in the schools under the mentorship of a current teacher with whose guidance they learn new skills and test theory. The bond between the student and the cooperating teacher is strong: Cooperating teachers introduce interns to the reality of students, resources, classes, schedules, and the many complex issues of the teacher's role. They assign teaching responsibilities to the interns, provide effective daily developmental supervision, and play a direct role in evaluation.

As the College of Education redefined its goals for the internship, it decided to introduce the professional portfolio as the predominant means by which student interns trace their professional growth as educators. The goals for students in internships are the following:

- Develop and refine teaching skills and personal teaching styles

- Become aware of and accept the full responsibilities of a teacher

- Become self-analytical and self-evaluative of teaching capabilities

- Meet the school-based experiences requirement for teacher certification

All interns are introduced to the concept of professional portfolios at their orientation to internships. They are provided with an overview of the process of portfolio development (see Part IV of this volume), including a model presented on video, and are invited to follow up by assembling their own. The following description of the portfolio and its goals is taken from the college web site (http://www.usask.ca/education/csbe/portfolio.htm).

> Most people are familiar with the idea of an artist's portfolio, a collection of the best, authentic examples of the artist's own artistic expression. For teachers, a portfolio is a collection of authentic, learner-specific artifacts that give evidence of one's growth and development as a teacher. It should reflect that an intern/teacher's development continues over time and that professional development is an individualized process. Typically, it is a relatively short document of materials that summarize and highlight the character of the teacher.

The reasons for promoting the use of professional portfolios are: the professional portfolio is widely recognized as a tool for self-evaluation and self-reflection, resulting in the improvement of instruction; the self-reflective process initiated by the portfolio sets the stage for a career of continuing professional development; the constructive process of assembling a portfolio can enhance collegial discussion; and a professional portfolio used when seeking employment can improve a candidate's likelihood of being hired.

Unlike the case for dietetics and agriculture students, participation in the process is entirely voluntary for education students and is not linked to the evaluation of the internship. Almost all students, however, begin the process.

Education's professional portfolio is a structured way to record reflections as responsibility for teaching a class increases. While the process of portfolio creation is important to the college, the product itself is becoming increasingly important to the students to showcase their skills for job searches.

The professional portfolio process in education has not been systematically evaluated yet. However, the anecdotal evidence from students, school board directors, and superintendents suggests that the interns who create experiential learning portfolios while they are on their major practicum and who continue to add to these portfolios during the rest of their time at university can articulate their achievements, goals, and philosophies of teaching much more impressively.

The portfolio is also having a spillover effect into the professional practice of the mentors who, seeing the value of the process for student interns, begin to compile their own portfolios.

WHAT CAN WE CONCLUDE FROM THE THREE EXAMPLES?

The growing emphasis on experiential learning in professional programs has necessitated changes in assessment:

- From sole emphasis on the products or outcomes to a concern for the process

- From passive response to active construction of meaning

- From simple acquisition to an emphasis on metacognition

- From an accumulation of isolated facts and skills to an emphasis on the application and use of knowledge

- From single occasion assessment to samples over time

(Adapted from Herman, Aschbacker & Winters, 1992)

Many of our assessment tools focus on the product, a focus inappropriate in the three examples provided. Few assessment tools emphasize the process that helps to embed the knowledge, put it into context, and give the student more ownership and control. Experiential learning portfolios do exactly that.

Portfolios involve students in the assessment process: managing and monitoring their learning in both the cognitive and affective domains, documenting their progress and achievement over time, articulating their achievement levels, and more importantly, experiencing success. Portfolios also encourage students to embark on the cycle of lifelong learning. As they reflect on whether they have achieved their learning objectives, students can actually convert gaps into new objectives and establish new learning plans by engaging in the following processes:

- Clarifying values, learning objectives, and goals

- Assessing skills

- Translating gaps into learning objectives or opportunities

- Selecting appropriate learning activities

- Identifying and using resources

- Developing evaluation strategies for continuous growth

(Adapted from Whitaker & Breen, 1996)

Experiential learning portfolios also simplify the task for the assessor by making the learning objectives and assessment criteria clear. As Simosko (1988) says,

> The assessor of experiential learning must focus only on the outcomes of the learning. Since he or she is not responsible for providing the instruction and has no control over the manner or time in which the learning took place, the good assessor must consider the discipline or course material as a whole and determine both what is

> most important and how best to assess those factors in the student's achievement. (p. 63)

In all three of the examples presented, college faculty redesigning courses realized that an experiential learning portfolio is the best assessment tool available to them. The portfolio is more than just a repository of work samples. It must rigorously reflect both the quality and quantity of work required by the curriculum, and in some cases by professional bodies, and the work that students are expected to produce to demonstrate that they have met the criteria.

The examples, too, share common goals: to bridge the gap between the classroom and experiential learning and to create a climate for student success in both. Teachers play a pivotal role in this process: They help by articulating clearly the objectives for the learning situation and by asking the students to become partners in the process.

The intentionality in the process of portfolio creation helps students not just to have an experience, but rather actively to construct meaning from it. Such reflection and self-analysis needed for the creation of an experiential learning portfolio can turn the student from a tourist to a traveler, according to a distinction made by Damarian (1993). A tourist and a traveler can visit the same city but leave it with different outcomes. A tourist will try to see all of the sights, learn their names, take lots of pictures, eat lots of the local cuisine, and observe the citizens perform their rituals. A traveler, on the other hand, will seek to understand the city, to know and live with the people, to understand their languages and culture, to participate in the rituals of the city. At the University of Saskatchewan's Colleges of Agriculture, Pharmacy and Nutrition, and Education, the experiential learning portfolio ensures that students are more than tourists.

ACKNOWLEDGMENTS

Shawna Berenbaum, associate professor and head, Division of Dietetics, College of Pharmacy and Nutrition, University of Saskatchewan; Lynne Bayne, administrative coordinator, Centre for School-Based Experiences, College of Education, University of Saskatchewan; Pauline Molder, manager, Experiential Education Program, College of Agriculture, University of Saskatchewan.

REFERENCES

Damarian, S. K. (1993). School and situated knowledge: Travel or tourism? *Educational Technology, 33* (3), 27–32.

Herman, J. L., Aschbacker, P., & Winters, L. (1992). *A practical guide to alternative assessment.* Alexandria, VA: Association for Supervision and Curriculum Development.

Hutchings, P., & Wutzdorff, A. (1988). Experiential learning across the curriculum: Assumptions and principles. In P. Hutchings & A. Wutzdorff (Eds.), *Knowing and doing: Learning through experience* (pp. 5–19). San Francisco, CA: Jossey-Bass.

Nelson, C. (2001). Nelson's notebook. *National Teaching & Learning Forum, 10* (4), 10–11.

Simosko, S. (1988). *Assessing experiential learning.* In J. H. MacMillan (Ed.), *Assessing students' learning* (pp. 61–71). San Francisco, CA: Jossey Bass.

Whitaker, U., & Breen, P. (1996). *Bridging the gap: A learner's guide to transferable skills.* San Francisco, CA: The Learning Center.

Wong, A. T. (1999). *Prior learning assessment and recognition: A guide for university faculty and administrators.* Saskatoon, Canada: University of Saskatchewan, University Extension Press.

Using Electronic Portfolios for the Improvement of Teaching and Learning

Dennis M. Holt and Paula McAllister
University of North Florida

The College of Education and Human Services at the University of North Florida (UNF) has established a pre-service teacher education program that emphasizes portfolio assessment coupled with clinical experiences in school classrooms. At UNF, portfolio assessment is defined as the practice of collecting data to make decisions on the progress of pre-service teachers and their students as the pre-service teachers develop their understanding of teaching and acquire skill in facilitating student learning. Clinical education is the organized and supervised program of school-based teaching and learning experiences which serves gradually to induct pre-service teachers into the profession of teaching.

PORTFOLIOS AND CLINICAL EXPERIENCES

In the freshman year, pre-service teachers complete their first portfolio for EDF 1005—Introduction to Education. Details of the requirements for their portfolios are contained in the course syllabus. The 18-hour clinical education component of the course provides pre-service teachers with supervised observations and limited teaching experiences that enable them to apply what they are learning through supervised classroom experiences with students in school settings.

In their sophomore year, students complete EME 2040—Introduction to Educational Technology. A portfolio of technology products linked to teaching tasks is required. Details of the course requirements are contained in the course syllabus.

111

During the completion of 100 hours of clinical experience through two two-semester-hour field laboratory courses in the junior year, pre-service teachers prepare working portfolios through which they document their work with students in classroom settings. These working portfolios contain collections of carefully developed artifacts and documents used to portray their professional growth. A CD-ROM disk is produced to guide the development of their portfolios (Boulware & Holt, 1998). Details of the requirements are contained in the course syllabi.

The culminating experience of the teacher education program is a 16-week internship, during which each pre-service teacher produces a professional portfolio. The portfolios are a selective and streamlined collection of teaching and learning materials that include documentation of their mastery of Florida's 12 pre-professional accomplished practices (Florida Education Standards Commission, 1996). A CD-ROM is produced to guide the development of the portfolios (Holt, 2001). Details of the requirements for internship and portfolio development are contained in the internship handbook. A textbook on portfolios provides a helpful guide to portfolio development (Campbell, Cignetti, Melenyzer, Nettles, & Wyman, 2001).

EXAMPLES OF ELECTRONIC PORTFOLIOS

Over the years, several pre-service teachers have produced electronic portfolios that were an outgrowth of their interest in educational technology and the portfolio assessment process. Computer software by IBM, Macromedia, Read, and Microsoft was used to produce the electronic portfolios. Multimedia creation stations were assembled to provide computer hardware and additional software to support the work.

The multimedia creation stations used to produce the CD-ROM–based electronic portfolios include powerful multimedia personal computers with large RAM, hard drives, and stereo sound. They also include read/write CD-ROM recorder/players; digital capture cards; color scanners; digital still cameras; camcorders; video capture cards to convert analog video from a video camera or VCR to compressed video for storage; large storage devices for graphics, sound, and video, including Zip drives (Iomega); software to accompany the hardware, including Photoshop (Adobe); and software for pre- and post-production digital design. The pre-service teachers' documents are created in Word (Microsoft) and the CD-ROMs created in Director (Macromedia). See illustrations from Dana Bennazar's and Erin Claxton's electronic portfolios in Part III of this volume.

The portfolio system, HyperPortfolio published by Read Media, Inc., is used with UNF pre-service teachers to produce electronic portfolios. The results are very promising. The CD-ROM and Internet compatible system includes detailed instructor and student manuals to guide the production of multimedia portfolios (Read & Cafolla, 1999).

ELECTRONIC PORTFOLIOS WITH K–12 ELECTRONIC PROJECTS

Over the past seven years, the authors have facilitated several teaching and learning projects in collaboration with schools and business partners. Throughout the projects, pre-service teachers develop an understanding of appropriate uses for educational technology in school-based professional development classrooms (Holt & McAllister, 1997; Holt & McAllister, 1999; Holt, Ludwick, & McAllister, 1996; Holt, McAllister, & Ingram, in press).

During each year of the projects, pre-service teachers guide the development of students' electronic projects that document achievement gains in academic areas such as art, language arts, mathematics, science, and social studies. The students' electronic projects link to the pre-service teachers' electronic portfolios. Selected computer courseware, software, and multimedia computers are effectively employed to enable the pre-service teachers and their students to display their work. Two examples of such projects are described and illustrated below.

EXAMPLE 1: LONE STAR 2000

The Lone Star 2000 project was a five-year collaboration between Lone Star Elementary School of the Duval County Public Schools in Jacksonville, Florida; the Division of Curriculum and Instruction of the College of Education and Human Services at the University of North Florida; and business partners, including the IBM Corporation, Logical Business Solutions, Inc., and AT&T Broadband (formerly MediaOne and now Comcast). Lone Star 2000 was designed to improve teaching and learning skills in college and K–12 classrooms through the use of educational technologies.

During the fifth year, five Lone Star Elementary School teachers, a science resource teacher, five UNF teaching interns, a UNF professor, and a LBS technology educator participated in the project. Three of the teaching interns were assigned to first-grade classrooms, one to a third-grade classroom, and one to a fourth-grade classroom.

Early in the semester, the pre-service teachers received two days of training in the use of IBM educational courseware. Topics covered during the two-day training included Teaching and Learning with Computers (TLC), an IBM approach to classroom instruction, an introduction to IBM science and language arts instructional courseware, and training in a multimedia authoring system. A month later, the interns received a third day of training in the specific details of electronic portfolio development.

Training consisted of hands-on instruction in the use of IBM computers, a large-screen projection device, and curriculum-based IBM courseware, including *Write Along, Stories and More II, The Nature of Science–Through the Woods,* and *LinkWay Live!,* a multimedia authoring tool. The pre-service teachers learned to use IBM educational technology to present whole class lessons to students and IBM's Teaching and Learning with Computers (TLC) techniques for utilizing the computers for pair and small-group learning center instruction. In addition, they learned how to use *Write Along* and *LinkWay Live!* to produce electronic portfolios creatively and direct the development of linked electronic folders of student work.

The focus for this project was on using technology to present integrated language arts and science curricula to students in innovative, dynamic ways and on documenting student learning through personal electronic portfolios linked to student electronic folders. The emphasis was on direct, simplified training for interns and the efficient application and transfer of skills to their students. As a special feature, Jack Neilly, a local author, donated copies of his book *Larry the Lightning Bug and the Lighthouse Adventure* to the students in the five participating classrooms. The book was used as part of the integrated language arts and science focus of the project. At the conclusion of the project, Neilly participated in a "Technology Sharing and Meet the Author" event for students, parents, interns, and teachers. Illustrations from Annette Collins's electronic portfolio work in the project are included in Part III of this volume.

EXAMPLE 2: TECHNOLOGY 2000

The Technology 2000 project was a collaboration between the University of North Florida; Chets Creek and Lone Star elementary schools of the Duval County Public School District; and Logical Business Solutions, Inc., a business partner. The project was designed to improve teaching and learning through the use of educational technologies and included the production of electronic folders linked to the electronic portfolios of pre-service teachers. Participants in the project included a University of North Florida professor who served as project director, a business partner technology trainer, five University of North Florida pre-service teachers, five directing teachers from Chets Creek and Lone Star elementary schools, two school principals, a media specialist, and 110 students from three first-grade, one third-grade, and one fifth-grade classrooms. Throughout the project, pre-service teachers developed the ability to use computers and related technology to enhance their classroom instruction significantly. Their students learned to use technology to demonstrate academic achievement and computer skills.

The pre-service teachers learned to use educational technology, including laptop and desktop computers, scanners, digital still cameras, and video cameras for creating presentations and for instructional activities. They learned to use courseware, software, and related technology-based materials available at the schools for classroom instruction, assessment, and evaluation, with an emphasis on IBM's Teaching and Learning with Computers (TLC) approach to instruction. They became knowledgeable about available technologies for use with a single computer to present whole-class instruction, while successfully conducting technology-infused lessons. They used the multimedia presentation tool of PowerPoint (Microsoft) to create instructional materials that incorporated text, video, sound, and graphics. Through the use of PowerPoint, each of their students created electronic folders that demonstrated the achievement of learning outcomes. As one means of demonstrating the success of their instruction, student electronic folders were linked to the electronic portfolios of each participating pre-service teacher. Illustrations from Lindsay Perani's electronic portfolio are included in Part III of this volume.

CONCLUSION

Portfolios can be used effectively to guide the development of pre-service teachers and the students they teach. Through electronic portfolios, especially, such as those we have demonstrated in our samples, both pre-service teachers and students can document their mastery of education standards. They can also provide evidence of personal growth and development.

References

Boulware, Z., & Holt, D. (1998). Using CD-ROM technology with preservice teachers to develop portfolios. *T.H.E. Journal, 26* (2), 60–62.

Campbell, D. H., Cignetti, P. B., Melenyzer, B. J., Nettles, D. H., & Wyman, R. M., Jr. (2001). *How to develop a professional portfolio: A manual for teachers* (2nd ed.). Boston, MA: Allyn and Bacon.

Florida Education Standards Commission. (1996). Accomplished, professional, and pre-professional competencies for teachers of the 21st century. Tallahassee, FL: Florida Department of Education. Retrieved from http://coe.fgcu.edu/Faculty/Honeychurch/ap/apindex.htm

Holt, D. (2001). Using CD-ROM to guide the development of professional portfolios. *Proceedings of SITE 2001,* 1442–1446.

Holt, D., Ludwick, K., & McAllister, P. (1996). Lone Star 2000: Documenting successful school or university teaching and learning. *T.H.E. Journal, 24* (3), 77–81.

Holt, D., & McAllister, P. (1997). Lone Star 2000: Soaring into the future with technology. (ERIC Document Reproduction Service No. ED 400780)

Holt, D., & McAllister, P. (1999). Lone Star 2000: Technology for today. *Proceedings of SITE 1999,* 1029–1034.

Holt, D., McAllister, P., & Ingram, E. (in press). Technology 2000: Using electronic portfolios for the performance assessment of teaching and learning. *Computers in the Schools, 18* (4).

Read, D., & Cafolla, R. (1999). Multimedia portfolios for pre-service teachers: From theory to practice. *Journal of Technology and Teacher Education, 7* (2), 97–113

Portfolio Design: The Basics

Jeannette Hung
Dalhousie University

WHAT

What Is a Career Portfolio?

A portfolio is a collection of documents, artifacts, or materials which are representative of your academic, leisure, and career development activities. Each portfolio is tailored to a particular purpose, such as organizing your own thinking about your career development. As well, it can assist in the presentation of your qualifications, skills, experience, and achievements, especially to employers and admission committees. Carefully selected and constructed, your portfolio is a concrete reflection of who you are, who you hope to become, and what you hope to achieve in your career and personal development.

A portfolio is a process as well as a product. As a process, it requires you to identify and reflect upon what motivates and satisfies you. You examine and present your interests, skills values, needs, goals, and strategies. Much of the power of your portfolio comes from this process. As a product, it requires a concrete collection of documents that evidence your work and learning history, skills, interests, abilities, and feedback from others.

WHY

Why Create a Career Portfolio?

Career portfolios are frequently used for interviews. However, a career portfolio is more than just a thick folder for your job search. It is a carefully organized synthesis of your accomplishments, learning, and goals.

In the process of creating your portfolio, you will discover a greater understanding of what you have to offer an employer, so you will be more effective in your job search. When you are more effective in your job search, you will be more confident with risk taking and career decision-making.

With more confidence, you will find more opportunities, and this increases your ability to market yourself and to network more effectively.

Ultimately, you will increase your chances of a successful and meaningful career, one that reflects your interests and the things that are important to you.

How

What Form Does a Career Portfolio Take?

A career portfolio is usually presented in a zippered case, a three-ring binder, or a multimedia format. The print documents are organized with dividers, tabs, labels, and plastic sheet protectors that are useful for holding documents and work samples. A digital format often contains text used in combination with audio and video files.

Each portfolio is tailored to a specific purpose and audience and should include:

- Statements of philosophy—what you value and contribute to your work, your work standards, your interests and objectives

- Evidence of your accomplishments

- Proof of things you have done—work samples, publications

- Academic transcripts or skills transcripts, letters of reference, performance evaluations, certificates

- Scholarships or other awards received

- Memberships obtained

- Involvement in community service or service to the university

- Your résumé or curriculum vitae

  Each portfolio should include records of achievement:

- Presentations

- Writing samples

- Research grants/proposals

- Works in progress

- Artwork

- Slides

- CDs
- Photography
- Performances

Each portfolio should include descriptions of your skills:

- Leadership
- Communication
- Marketing
- Computer
- Teamwork
- Interests

Each portfolio should include records of extracurricular activities:

- Athletics
- Student societies
- Campus media or politics
- Community service projects
- Volunteer work

Depending on the audience, you may want to include a statement of originality and confidentiality to protect your documents from unauthorized duplication.

TIPS

General Tips

- Have a clear purpose (tailored to your audience).
- Ensure it is attractive (the visual presentation will reflect your professional standards).
- Sequence the contents (in order of importance to your audience).
- Design each section so it is easy to scan (use lots of white space, consistent font, style and spacing, and tab extenders).
- Present each page clearly. Ensure it is grammatically correct and error free.

- Add explanatory footnotes to work samples.

- Use clear sheet protectors (nonglare sheet protectors are not as clear or crisp).

- Remove materials as they lose their relevance.

- Seek advice and feedback from friends, colleagues, instructors, supervisors, or a career counselor.

- Have a backup copy.

Evaluating Your Portfolio

- Are your philosophy and purpose statements supported by your sections?

- Is your collection aesthetically pleasing?

- Can your audience easily see your accomplishments and the contributions you could make?

- Have you presented yourself at your best? Do you need some help with your self-assessments?

- Have you included comments or evaluations on your performance? Can you accurately predict what people would say about your work?

- Have you made strategic use of your collection for gap analysis? Do you know the areas you need to work on? Do you have a plan to fill in those gaps?

- Does your portfolio reflect your usual work standards? Is the collection itself a typical work sample?

Use of Reflective Writing/Learning Portfolios in a Junior-Level Water Resources Engineering Class

Randall L. Kolar and David A. Sabatini
University of Oklahoma

THE SETTING

In fall 2000, the learning portfolio strategy of reflective writing was used as part of the overall assessment protocol in CE 3212: Environmental Engineering I (EEI), our junior-level water resources engineering course required for all civil and environmental engineering majors at the University of Oklahoma. EEI is a core course in the Sooner City curriculum[1]; consequently, students are faced with designing the primary components of the city's water delivery system (water source, pumps, storage, and distribution lines), the city's sanitary sewer system (gravity and/or force mains), and the storm water management system.

In the course we promote active learning via a variety of individual and group assignments (where the groups are permanent), ranging from virtual experiments to discussions on current events in water resources. Also, we team teach the course, but rather than a tag team approach, we are both present in every class. Grades for the course are based on a weighted average of engineering design assignments, RATs[2], reflective writing essays, and the final exam. In academic year 2000–2001, reflective writing essays counted for 10% of the total grade.

Because of the nature of the design material in the course, and because we desire to help students see the big picture early (which helps motivate their learning), we use the just-in-time learning paradigm wherein the Sooner City design tasks are given to the students at the beginning of the semester. In the remainder of the year, class activities (short lectures, class discussions, group exercises, or outside reading assignments) are driven by what the students need to know in order to complete the specified task.

Enrollment in the course is typically on the order of 45 to 50 students. As required by the College of Engineering, all students own laptop computers with wireless network cards, thus allowing each class to be a networked computing lab.

THE ROLE OF REFLECTIVE WRITING IN EEI

Having team taught this course since 1998, we have noticed that students are simultaneously excited and daunted by the real world nature of the design tasks and the many decisions that must be made along the path, decisions that require good engineering judgment. However, students rarely posses such judgment; it must be learned through practice, presenting us with the paradox of how to learn engineering design without having good judgment (that in itself requires practice at engineering design). If this sounds confusing, one can imagine how young engineers feel. Because the course is often students' first exposure to design, that by nature is a very open-ended process without a unique solution, and due to the just-in-time delivery of class material, students are quickly forced out of their comfort zone. Under such circumstances, students have often complained that exams do not adequately reflect all that they have learned. We agree.

As we studied the design projects and our learning objectives, we saw a need to engage students in their learning progress in a different way, that of the learning portfolio's key strategy of reflective writing. Reflective writing affords students the opportunity to look back on their work and summarize their progress toward learning goals such as good design principles. In doing so, they are more likely to keep the material in perspective. Also, reflective writing provides an effective feedback mechanism for the instructors as we progress through the course material.

Furthermore, one of the objectives of the Sooner City project is to get students to see the complete picture—that is, to view civil engineering not as a collection of specialized, independent courses but as an integrated whole. This type of thinking is difficult to assess with traditional academic tools (quizzes, exams, homework problems). Reflective writing as part of a total learning portfolio is a tool that can be used to assess student progress toward grasping the big picture.

What do we mean by reflective writing? With help from our colleague in the Instructional Development Program, Dr. L. D. Fink, we drew a distinction between substantive writing, where students focus their attention on information and ideas about the subject, and reflective writing that calls for students to focus on the learning experience itself. To do this, students try to understand and write about the significance and meaning of a personal learning experience. Hence, in this kind of writing, it is quite acceptable and appropriate for students to address very personal issues, such as "Was this fun, interesting, exciting?" "Did this make sense to me?" "How did it connect with my previous knowledge or beliefs about this subject or with my ideas on other subjects?"

To explain the use of reflective writing in the context of an engineering course, and to assist students in preparing their learning portfolios, we put together a detailed handout (available in Part IV of this volume). All writing assignments were completed on the web, allowing us to read them quickly and provide timely feedback via email. Also, at the end of the semester, the students' writing assignments were bound along with their design work to form a complete learning portfolio for the course. Questions we asked students to consider included the following:

- What key ideas or information have you learned about water resources engineering?

- What have you learned about how to use or apply the technical content of this course?

- What have you been able to integrate within or external to this course?

- What have you learned about the human dimension of the subject either regarding yourself and/or your interaction with others?

- What have you learned about how to learn?

OUR OBSERVATIONS ON LEARNING PORTFOLIO EFFICACY

The results of our first foray into reflective writing were both gratifying and exciting. The vast majority of the class took the reflective writing assignment seriously and turned in papers that were satisfying to read as teachers. The portfolios helped us see that our efforts as teachers had not been pointless.

More importantly, however, this kind of writing helped students themselves become more engaged in their own learning. By reflecting and writing about their own learning experience throughout the course, they became more self-conscious of themselves as learners and thereby became more ready to take charge of their own learning. By the end of the course, they had a fuller picture of what they had learned and the significance of that learning.

Also, recall that one of the reasons for using learning portfolios was to help us assess students' progress toward grasping the big picture, that is, how the material in this course fits into the overall Sooner City infrastructure design. In the past, when we did not use reflective writing, progress toward this goal was difficult, if not impossible, to measure with traditional problem-solving exams. However, reflective writing encouraged students to examine and assess their ability to function as broadly educated civil engineers in the real world, allowing us to gauge their progress toward becoming mature engineers. Comments from the papers indicate that the majority of the students made great strides toward this goal, and they had fun doing it.

The following student remarks (with some minor grammatical corrections) extracted from the reflective writing assignments substantiate our observations. We note in particular that these are extremely mature statements about the design process, especially for juniors experiencing their first design tasks.

- At the beginning of the course, I was frustrated because designing is hard for me, especially when we are designing open-ended problems. It felt so overwhelming, like a person looking at a gigantic jigsaw puzzle not knowing where to begin. However, as we progressed as a class and as the professors got us familiar with the material, I began to develop interests in water and its uses.... But most important of all is that I feel that things I have learned in the past are coming together.

- As for open-ended design questions, I think these types of problems allow students to see the bigger picture, and they penalize us less because we can approach the open-ended problems with different methods that enable us to make use of our good engineering judgment.

- In closing, I feel that this course is both fun and very interesting, because designing open-ended problems really gave me an opportunity to try to put together the information that I have learned in the past.

- By giving us problems that are sometimes broad in scope or vague in detail, requiring some kind of logical assumptions, the course allows us to come up with real world solutions and begin to understand the big picture of total design.... Furthermore, the Sooner City design program and linking other classes to what we are doing are some of the greatest things I have seen, mainly due to the fact that in the real world, we will need to rely on [other] consultants for some of the design process. After taking this class, I think I will feel more comfortable with the idea of total design and how to approach a problem in the real world.

- Overall, I believe I came away from the course learning more than I had intended upon entering it. I figured it would be about preserving the environment and keeping things unpolluted, but it was not that at all, and I was glad to see that. I found this course more interesting than structural analysis, which means a lot since I am a structural engineer.

- It takes a lot of time to learn anything. Sometimes your best ideas don't work out as you hope. This just means that you need to look at several options from the beginning and narrow them down until you have the solution you need. In reality, there is rarely one answer to any given problem. Sometimes you should take others' opinions into consideration, but there are times when you should stick to your convictions. All in all, I'm surprised at how much I've learned in this class.

CONCLUSION

Our first experience with reflective writing in a learning portfolio leads us to believe it was a success. Reflective writing not only provided us with valuable feedback for assessing our course and curriculum objectives, but also promoted students' self-awareness of the learning process and required them to assume responsibility for their own learning objectives. We definitely plan to continue and, if possible, expand upon the practice of having students engage in reflective writing and develop learning portfolios in this and other courses.

Endnotes

1) Sooner City refers to a comprehensive curriculum reform project in which students are charged with designing the major infrastructure components for this virtual city, beginning in the freshman year. Among other things, a common design task promotes lateral and vertical integration of the curriculum and higher level thinking skills. A full description of the project is in paper by Kolar, et al. (2000, January). *Journal of Engineering Education, 89* (1), 79–87.

2) RATs stands for Readiness Assessment Tests, which, as the name implies, are quizzes to assess the preparedness of students for new material. RATs are short

announced quizzes over a reading assignment (text and/or handouts). They are given at the beginning of each major topical area before any class time is spent on the material. The same RAT is taken first by individuals and then by groups, followed by a class discussion. RATs typically consist of true/false and multiple-choice questions that test understanding of basic concepts; they rarely contain computational-type problems. We believe they serve a number of purposes, including preparing students for class, freeing up class time for more complex engineering issues, fostering both self-learning and team building, and guiding class discussion. All RATs are closed book.

The Math Student Course Portfolio

Ted Panitz
Cape Cod Community College

During the semester, students in my math courses develop a variety of study methods and class materials that they use to understand the course concepts, study for exams, and complete other requirements. They often treat each activity as a separate and independent action. A course learning portfolio is a mechanism designed to help students organize their materials into a unified and interrelated approach to the course. In addition, this exercise provides an alternative means of communication between the student and professor and may serve to provide a warning if the student is having difficulties or problems with class procedures. In the following paragraphs, I include excerpts from materials I have developed on the use of learning portfolios in my math courses. More extensive and detailed information is found in Panitz (2001) and online at http://home.capecod. net/~tpanitz/ewacbook/ch12.html.

I introduce the course portfolio during the final third of the semester as an alternative form of assessment instead of relying on the standard hour exams. I encourage students to include in their portfolios any materials that will help them demonstrate to me that they understand and can apply the course concepts. I provide a list of suggested items and encourage students to use their imagination. Materials generated through group activities are acceptable. One item that is required is the chapter exam. It is used to promote individual accountability and counts as an important element of the portfolio.

SAMPLE CONTENTS

Here is a representative sample table of contents for a math course learning portfolio:

1) Chapter Test

2) Chapter Test Corrected

3) Chapter Homework

4) Review Sheet with Necessary Formulas

5) Writing Assignments

- Book section on how to solve word problems

- Poetry in math

- How did the quadratic equation come to be a short story?

6) In-Class Group Assignments

7) Sample Test Developed by the Group and Answers to Sample Test

8) Flash Cards Used for Studying Important Formulas and Procedures

9) Reflections, Observations, and Comments About Personal Performance, Problems, and Successes During Classes

10) Questions That Occur After Class or When Doing Homework

The portfolio is intended to broaden and expand the information I have available to evaluate student performance. The chapter exam serves as the starting point in the evaluation process. Next, in order to complete the evaluation, I look at homework assignments, in-class work, text or class notes, flash cards, course journal writing, and other assignments given during the semester period under consideration. I use all the information to assign a grade.

The process involves a certain amount of subjectivity because I do not quantify the grading of journal entries, as this would tend to limit students' imaginations. I use the journal evaluation to raise or lower chapter exam grades.

I assign the portfolio during the last third of the semester versus starting immediately because I want the students to become comfortable and familiar with class procedures such as writing assignments, collaborative learning activities, and many interactive class exercises. Also, by the last third of the semester, students will have accumulated a variety of materials that I can ask them to organize more effectively. Alternatively, of course, the portfolio could be assigned at the beginning of the semester. Regardless of timing, directions and opportunities for peer and instructor feedback result in stronger portfolios. (Part IV of this volume contains a portfolio assignment

I use in my math courses to help offer direction in assessing students' mastery levels.)

Students find the portfolio concept of evaluation encouraging and helpful. They appreciate how, in addition to teaching them how to organize their materials, the portfolio gives them an opportunity to demonstrate their competence in a variety of ways. In math courses, especially, where there is a high level of anxiety, students are enthusiastic about communicating how they have spent their time working on course content. They prefer a grading system that is not based solely on 50-minute exams.

PURPOSES OF THE COURSE LEARNING PORTFOLIO

The course learning portfolio serves several purposes:

1) Provides information to the professor that enables a more complete student assessment and grading process

2) Helps students organize a variety of course materials into a useful format

3) Encourages students to review all their course materials within a unified context

4) Allows students to demonstrate course proficiency through a variety of mechanisms

5) Provides an avenue of communication between the professor and student during the semester

ALTERNATE USES

1) Students review previous work completed during the semester in preparation for the final exam.

2) Students develop a portfolio of materials to bring forward to the next course.

3) The portfolio provides information for employment purposes. The material may be used as part of a résumé or as backup documentation.

OPPORTUNITIES FOR COLLABORATIVE LEARNING

Finally, portfolios have several implications and applications for collaborative learning opportunities that foster peer mentoring and that enhance learning:

1) Groups develop a list of items that would be appropriate for inclusion in the portfolio.

2) Groups develop a master list of portfolio items through a whole class consideration of each group's suggestions.

3) Groups develop grading criteria for the portfolios, including quantity of materials, quality levels, grade assignment.

4) Groups or pairs review each other's portfolios for completeness and whether they meet the grading criteria.

REFERENCE

Panitz, T. (2001). *Learning together: Keeping teachers and students actively involved by writing across the curriculum.* Stillwater, OK: New Forums Press.

The Kalamazoo Portfolio

Zaide Pixley
Kalamazoo College

The original "K" Plan of 1963 sought to increase experiential learning at the undergraduate level by incorporating it into its curriculum career internships, rigorous academic study abroad, and senior individualized projects. In the last four decades, students who graduated from Kalamazoo College have done extraordinary things. Although they have been able to build excellent credentials, the greatest benefit to our students is derived from fully integrating experiential opportunities into academic course work, rather than simply accumulating independent experiences. Given the complex nature of a Kalamazoo education, students needed a way to gain a deeper understanding of the significance of what they have done and to weave their possibly disparate experiences into a unified whole.

ACHIEVING LEARNING TASKS

The Kalamazoo Portfolio is intended to address this need. It provides students with a vehicle to achieve several learning tasks:

- Track and interpret their accomplishments in and out of the classroom

- Draw connections among their activities and achievements

- Record experiences they might otherwise forget or undervalue

- Increase their levels of self-understanding and confidence

- See patterns emerging in their areas of study and interest

FACILITATING GOALS

The portfolio is designed to facilitate the following goals:

- Bring a greater clarity of purpose and a higher level of motivation to the classroom

- Demonstrate students' competencies and capabilities as they pursue internships, leadership positions on campus and in the community, or field-based research experiences

- Demonstrate students' competency with computer-based technologies

- Help students to be proactive in designing their educational plans and pursuing post-graduate opportunities

Because of Kalamazoo's emphasis on character education, what is called the dimensions of a "K" education became part of the portfolio: lifelong learning, career readiness, leadership, intercultural understanding, and social responsibility. The portfolio was also intended to link each student's program of study directly to the college's mission of providing "enlightened leadership to a richly diverse and increasingly complex world."

Two final things made the portfolio possible: the advent of the nonlinear and endlessly connecting web, which made such linkages not only possible but interesting, and a change of calendar and curriculum. In fall 1996 Kalamazoo became one of the first colleges to adopt an electronic portfolio, a project soon funded by FIPSE (Fund for Improving Post-Secondary Education).

STRUCTURE AND PURPOSE

In the course of its implementation, the portfolio has undergone several refinements. For example, a committee on experiential education—consisting of faculty, administrators, and students—spent a considerable amount of time discussing the concept and revising the structure of the portfolio in the fourth year of its implementation. The resulting framework builds the portfolio into the parts of a Kalamazoo education where reflecting, analyzing, and setting goals are already taking place. Departments can choose to go beyond the minimalist college-wide requirements and transform portfolios for their majors into tailor-made, career-readiness tools.

FOUNDATIONS ESSAY

Students who intend to enroll at Kalamazoo are asked the summer before their matriculation to write a foundations essay. The essay is intended to encourage new students to put into words their hopes, plans, and goals for college. It helps advisors and peer leaders (student mentors) get to know the background and ambitions of the students they are advising or mentoring. Student mentors are asked to make comments in response to what enrolling

Table 1

The Kalamazoo Portfolio Framework

Year	Portfolio entry	What it is	Who responds
First Year	Foundations essay	Connects high school experience with the dimensions and skills* and sets goals for the first year	Advisors and peer leaders
	Portfolio creation and writing self-assessment	Creation of home page, writing self-assessment, link to best Seminar paper, link to Foundations Essay	First-year seminar faculty and portfolio consultants
	Academic goals and plan of study	Looks forward to sophomore year, declaration of major and study abroad	Advisors
Sophomores	Declaration of major	Brief description of preparation and goals for the major	Registrar, to departments
	Foundations for intercultural understanding	a) Essay questions for study abroad application, or b) reflection on experience with another culture in the US or abroad, or c) course work	a) International programs staff, or (a and b) portfolio office
Juniors	Reflection on career readiness	Résumé and a) reflection on career internship, or b) completion of career "Readiness Barometer" or other reflective piece	a) Career advisors, or b) portfolio office
	SIP contract	Brief description of preparation and goals for the SIP	SIP advisors
Seniors	Senior Connections Essay**	Connects various parts of "K" education, reflects on SIP, discusses growth in dimensions and skills*	Portfolio office, major department, or assessment committee

*Dimensions: lifelong learning, career readiness, leadership, intercultural understanding, social responsibility.

*Skills: information literacy, quantitative reasoning, writing, and oral communication

**Some departmentally approved capstone assignments or application essays may be substituted* FOR THE SENIOR CONNECTIONS ENTRY.

students have written, but not to assign a grade or correct the work. At the end of four years at Kalamazoo, the foundations essay helps students look back on the immense journey they have undertaken. The instructions read this way:

Foundations Essay

The **Foundations Essay** will become the first item in your Kalamazoo Portfolio. You can use it as a reference point as you make plans for international study, decide on a major, choose among internship opportunities, and engage in volunteer activities. In your senior year, as you write your **Senior Connections Essay**, you will be able to look back, see where you started, and make better connections among the parts of your "K" education. Build your essay around the *five dimensions* of a "K" education, which describe our view of an educated person—the kind of person we want to help you become. The *dimensions* will frame your college experiences.

The Dimensions

- An educated person is a *lifelong learner* who has found ways to develop and grow after the end of formal schooling and has a range of commitments and interests to be passionate about.

- An educated person is *socially responsible* and gives back to his or her community.

- An educated person possesses *intercultural understanding* and knows how to interact with people of various cultures and backgrounds.

- An educated person has explored his or her interests, strengths, and skills, and thus has developed *career readiness.*

- An educated person performs acts of *leadership* within his or her community, whether in a designated leadership position or behind the scenes.

Write a response (two to three double-spaced pages) in which you:

1) Choose two of these *dimensions* and connect them to your experiences before coming to college. Show how you have developed these *dimensions* in your academic work, community service, employment, travel, or other experiences that have been most influential. How have these activities and commitments made you who you are? How have they shaped what you think you might study, or what your range of interests is?

2) Select a third *dimension* that you would like to develop and describe why it will be important to your personal growth.

3) Finally, set two to three goals that you hope to achieve during your first year. What steps might be necessary to make these goals a reality?

WEB PAGE, LINKS TO BEST SEMINAR PAPER, WRITING SELF-ASSESSMENT

Throughout the fall term, students in first-year seminars (courses that focus on the development of writing and critical thinking) are asked to evaluate themselves as writers. Students have an opportunity to discuss their work with their instructor in writing conferences, gain critical feedback, and incorporate it into their own self-assessment. Each seminar uses one of its meetings for learning web design in workshops led by the portfolio coordinator and student portfolio consultants. New students are provided with technical help in creating their web pages (using Netscape Composer or Dreamweaver). At this session students link their foundations essays to their home pages and create links for their best seminar papers and writing self-assessments. As they master the art of making web pages and create a space where they can collect, compare, and reflect upon their best work, students learn more about themselves as critical thinkers and writers. The writing self-assessment rubric reads:

1) What are your strengths?

2) What are the areas in which you need to improve?

3) What steps will you take to develop your writing and thinking skills over the next four years? Base your assessment on comments on your

work by your first-year seminar instructor and peers and on your own experiences as a writer.

Later in the term, students can seek additional assistance from the portfolio coordinator and student portfolio consultants and attend ability-based workshops.

ACADEMIC GOALS AND PLAN OF STUDY

In spring of the freshman year, students are asked to plan the next year of study, a complicated process because they will need to prepare themselves for decisions concerning the sophomore year declaration of major and study abroad. The entry remains in their portfolios and provides a basis for future advising conversations and a check for the fulfillment of graduation requirements. Students are asked to address the following tasks:

1) Identify one or more potential majors, minors, or concentrations, and outline the sequence of courses needed to fulfill meet those requirements.

2) Describe the study abroad programs that you are most interested in.

3) Lay out potential sequences of courses for the next year, leading up to study abroad.

DECLARATION OF MAJOR

At Kalamazoo, students are encouraged to declare their majors before the end of their sophomore year, giving them time to work with their major departments before they leave for study abroad or internships. To encourage them to pull their thoughts about the major into sharper focus and give departments a picture of all the students declaring in that particular year, students are asked to address the following questions:

1) Why did you choose this particular major?

2) What in your background, course work, and life experience has prepared you for it?

3) How does this major support your personal and professional goals?

INTERCULTURAL UNDERSTANDING

Student portfolio writing has amply demonstrated that participation in study abroad is a pivotal and critical part of a Kalamazoo education. Nearly

85% of Kalamazoo students study abroad for at least a term in either the sophomore or junior year. To be admitted to particular programs, students must address the following points:

> Your motivation, preparation, and expectations for studying abroad are critical components in the evaluation of your application. The following questions are designed to help you consider the complexity of living in a new environment and how strongly our personal values and behavior are determined by the culture in which we live. We hope that you will consider the role of these cultural values when evaluating how well prepared you are for a cross-cultural experience and how you will continue preparing for your experience during the pre-departure orientation. Answer the following points in essay form and submit a paper copy with your program application:
>
> 1) Describe your motivations and reasons for choosing to apply for this particular study abroad program.
>
> 2) List your academic and intercultural goals for study abroad and how you will be able to achieve these goals in the program you have selected. Then, discuss how these goals will fit in with a liberal arts education and the five dimensions of the "K" Plan.
>
> 3) What values of your proposed host culture do you think will challenge you the most and why?

CAREER READINESS

In the sophomore or junior year, students taking internships through the Center for Career Development are asked to write a reflective paper that is linked to their portfolios. Papers are evaluated by career advisors (upperclass peer student mentors), who, in consultation with a professional staff member, respond to what the student has written and make suggestions for further career activities. Students receive these instructions:

Internship Reflective Paper

The final reflective paper is the primary method of demonstrating that your internship experience has been a process of significant learning.... While it is natural to be critical of your experience, remember that all experiences have learning value; focus on the impact of this experience and how it will benefit you in the future. The final evaluative paper should focus on:

1) The knowledge you obtained from your internship experience; highlight the strengths and challenges of your internship

2) How your internship experience relates to your coursework; a reflective commentary on various career options and related lifestyle issues

3) How your internship experience complements your "K" education and the five dimensions

The paper must summarize the following items:

1) How well you fulfilled your learning objectives (revisit the internship goals you listed on the program agreement and learning contract)

2) How your internship experience impacted your career decisions and how you see it impacting your decisions in the future

3) Actions you took to ensure a positive learning environment

Students who do not complete an internship arranged through the college center are asked to add their résumés to their portfolios and to complete a "Career Readiness Barometer" or another reflective piece about an experience that has helped prepare them for the workplace.

SENIOR INDIVIDUALIZED PROJECTS

A senior individualized project (SIP) is a personal research project that every Kalamazoo student is required to complete. To encourage students to pull their projects into a sharper focus, they are prompted to respond to the following instructions and questions:

1) Briefly describe your SIP

2) Then, address these questions:

   • How did you choose this particular SIP?

- How did any of the following influence your SIP choice: your major or minor, liberal arts courses, study abroad, internship or other experiences?

- How does this SIP support your personal and professional goals?

SENIOR CONNECTIONS ESSAY

The Kalamazoo Portfolio concludes with a senior connections essay that demonstrates a student's development and change over the four years of undergraduate education. Some departments (for example, English, history, psychology) devise their own highly effective assignments for reflective essays in senior seminars or other capstone courses. Applications to graduate or professional schools or for fellowships and grants can also be used. Senior connections essays are read and responded to by the student's major department and by members of the college's assessment committee. Students are given the following instructions:

Senior Connections Essay

What's next? We care about what you're going to do next and how what you've done at "K" has helped prepare you for employment, graduate school, or another endeavor. Your work on the portfolio has been intended to help you get ready: to see the connections between the disparate parts of a "K" education, collect your significant academic and experiential work in one place, learn web design, and develop long-term goals and plans that give coherence and direction to your education. The portfolio can also assist those of us who remain at the college. It can help advisors, faculty, and departments learn more about students interested in our disciplines and assess and improve our programs and curricula.

Your senior connections essay—your final portfolio entry—offers not only an account of what you have accomplished at Kalamazoo, but also your reflections on the ways in which you have grown as an individual. One of the best ways to demonstrate this growth is to comment on the interrelatedness of your educational experiences. What connections can you see among your favorite courses, your particular interests, and your developing proficiencies in certain fields? How have the courses you've taken at "K" intersected with your career development, study abroad, volunteer, leadership, or work experiences?

Structure your Senior Connections essay around these points:

1) What were the most significant parts of your Kalamazoo education? What did you learn from your major, other courses, study abroad and internship experiences, athletics, co-curricular activities, and SIP? Write about those most important to you.

2) How did these pursuits help you grow in the "K" dimensions (intercultural understanding, career readiness, social responsibility, leadership, lifelong learning,) and skills (oral and writing proficiency, information literacy, quantitative reasoning)? Choose those most important to you to discuss.

Sample Supplemental Entries

Students are encouraged to include other work in their portfolios, including some of the following:

1) Additional examples of outstanding work, selected by the student (best papers, key performances)

2) Departmentally designated assignments or projects

3) Symposia, conference, or SIP presentations (for example, the biology department presents its SIPs in an annual symposium, and the music department hosts a spring series of SIP recitals)

4) Letter of intent for graduate school

5) Application for job, fellowship, or grant

6) Integrative cultural research project or study abroad reflective essay (completed at the end of the experience)

7) Links to experiential education activities (service learning, campus organizations)

8) Application essays for leadership positions (resident advisor, peer leader, Academic Resource Center consultant)

9) Self-assessment by athletes with coaches

10) Other entries as designed by the student, including references to the importance of friends and family or links to other web sites (internships for Teach for America, for example)

RECOGNITION AND REWARDS

In order to be effective, portfolios must be integrated into the central educational goals and practices of an institution, and outstanding work must be recognized and made available as a model. At Kalamazoo, several students are awarded Marilyn J. LaPlante Senior Portfolio Awards, recognizing outstanding content and presentation, as well as attention to the critical elements and dimensions of the "K" Plan. Other awards in the sophomore and junior years highlight portfolios that focus on international understanding, career readiness, service learning, or campus leadership. Award-winning portfolios are posted on the college web site. The best reward for the portfolio, however, is the knowledge that someone the student respects has read and responded to each entry.

BENEFITS OF THE PORTFOLIO

At Kalamazoo, portfolios provide a number of benefits to students. They serve as a focal point of self-assessment, a place where students can see a record of progress, and a repository of their most significant work. The critical thinking and reflective writing that go into portfolios help students develop long-term goals and plans. The reflection asked for in the portfolio helps students give voice to their own understandings of their experiences—for example, that study abroad may not initially be the most fun a student has ever had, but it pays off in the long run. The position of portfolio consultants provides an excellent opportunity for students to engage in teaching and practice leadership skills.

To faculty and the institution as a whole, portfolios provide a big picture of undergraduate education. They enable departments and faculty to have a snapshot of their majors or advisees. They can aid in advising and decision-making processes and help advisors raise important questions with advisees. They provide a convenient way for faculty and departments to know more about students majoring, minoring, or participating in their disciplines, and for faculty to write more informed letters of recommendation. When portfolios are used consistently in departments and programs, they provide a way to assess and improve the departments. Finally, the range of experiences described in portfolios readily demonstrates the benefits of liberal learning.

THE ONGOING EVOLUTION OF THE KALAMAZOO PORTFOLIO

As the student population changes over the years, so do programs such as these. Future manifestations of the Kalamazoo Portfolio may include only four required gateway points: 1) the foundations essay before matriculation, 2) the creation of the web page and related links during the first term, 3) the rationale for the declaration of major, and 4) the final capstone senior connections essay, all points that are easily checked and verified. These would be supplemented by a number of recommended entries from which students could choose as appropriate and as they resonate with each student's experience. Efforts to keep the portfolio woven into the fabric of the educational experience must be consistently maintained. The issue of whether the portfolio is an add-on for students and faculty, or whether it actually enhances and deepens the educational experience, must be continually addressed. For more information, consult the Kalamazoo Portfolio web site at http://www.kzoo.edu/pfolio.

Increasing Student Comprehension Through Learning Portfolios in Archaeology: The Case of Caesarea Maritima in Israel

Farland Stanley
University of Oklahoma

During my teaching career, my interests have included the goal of strengthening students' skills and abilities in reading, writing, and critical thinking. My central motive has been to help students gain a fuller understanding of themselves, the world around them, and how the process and results of learning may lead to the enhancement of their lives. As a professor of classics and archaeology, I instruct courses that concern topics dealing with the civilizations of the ancient world. The topics in themselves have many opportunities to fulfill my teaching goals. However, in the process of teaching about the ancient Roman and Greek world, I believe that my students have especially profited from our University of Oklahoma archaeological expedition to Caesarea Maritima in Israel, a cooperative project with Combined Caesarea Expeditions, a consortium of international universities excavating the immense Roman harbor city some 45 kilometers north of Tel-Aviv.

On numerous occasions, as I have prepared my students for our departure to Caesarea, I have advised them that they were about to embark on an expedition that would recover materials from daily life in antiquity over 1,500 years ago. In addition to their excavation activities, I also inform them that I want them to participate in our learning portfolio project to help them relate better to what they will be learning specifically about their experiences. Approximately two weeks before we depart for Israel, I offer a brief historical overview of the history of Caesarea and inform students about what we will be doing with our learning portfolios.

In applying the learning portfolio concept to their educational experiences on site at Caesarea, students are encouraged as they excavate to be aware of initial impressions of all around them. I ask them to notice the actual physical terrain that they are exploring each day and to be aware of how it changes over the course of the excavation. I also ask them to observe the artifacts and structures that they discover on a daily basis and how these relate to what they learn about the cultures of the peoples who lived on the site. The instructions for such reflections in their learning portfolios are followed by the caution that after four weeks of excavation, their first impressions could be significantly altered, a learning curve that is captured well by the portfolio approach.

Finally, as the end of the four-week session approaches, I instruct students to reflect on the impressions of the experiences that they have acquired over time on site. After their reflections about and evaluation of their hands-on, experiential activities, they compose a paper for their portfolios that interprets their actual learning process and expresses what they feel they have learned or not learned and why they think the learning experience at Caesarea was important to them in either a positive or negative sense. I also ask them to comment specifically on how they think that the learning experience at Caesarea might have application to their approach to future learning objectives. Thus, to assist students in expressing what, how, and why they have learned, I pose a number of questions for them to address in their learning portfolios. Here is a sampling of the types of questions that become the core of students' portfolios:

1) Identify one experience that shows why you did or did not learn how to integrate what you learned at Caesarea with other realms of your life.

2) Identify one experience that shows why you did or did not acquire a better understanding of yourself as a learner.

3) What did you learn about the process of interacting with others which helps to complete a task?

4) Identify one experience that shows why you did or did not acquire a fuller understanding of how the learning process works through the discipline of archaeology.

5) What do you think you have learned about Near Eastern civilization which has application to your life?

Since 1990, Oklahoma students have joined almost 3,000 volunteers and staff who have collectively participated in the excavations at Caesarea, providing our students with an excellent learning opportunity. Incorporating learning portfolios for reflection and for application of knowledge has created an effective way for students to participate in reading, writing, and critical thinking exercises while also remaining engaged in the process of making practical, experiential discoveries at an actual archaeological excavation. Students take their observations, along with their firsthand experience in archaeological excavation, and reflect daily in written form about what they are discovering and learning overall. Their reflections include what they believe they have learned about archaeology and what they perceive has taken place in the learning process.

At the end of each excavation season, when I have completed reading the students' learning portfolios, I have been consistently pleased with what they learn and the way in which they reflect on their experiences. Without exception, all of the students express that their learning is enhanced and, for a few, the venture appears to have altered their career goals. Their portfolios uniformly reflect a careful, thoughtful attempt to analyze their summer experience and relate it to other areas of their learning. The final result of my own reflections on what I have learned from my work with students at Caesarea is that using the learning portfolio brings rich and rewarding returns.

If a key goal for teachers is continually to utilize methods that reinforce and sharpen reading, writing, and critical thinking, then the learning portfolio is a technique that has significant merit. It is one I will continue to use in the future to improve and assess students' learning in unique, experiential field work such as the archaeological excavations at Caesarea.

Interdisciplinary Effectiveness and the Learning Portfolio: Developing the Transferable Skills Required in the 21st Century Workplace

David A. Thomas
Arizona State University

SIGNIFICANT LEARNING: ONE EDUCATOR'S PERSPECTIVE

What skills and individual characteristics are most important if one hopes to excel in the 21st century workplace? How successful are our institutions of higher learning at helping students acquire these skills and individual characteristics? How can we, as educators, create an environment that helps students develop fundamental, transferable skills and become more effective learners?

My own experiences in the field and a growing body of organizational research suggest that recent college graduates typically lack many of the transferable skills most important for achieving success in the modern workplace: communication skills; interpersonal relations skills; flexibility and change receptivity; team skills; the ability to think across functional lines, to think interdisciplinarily; and the ability to learn effectively and improve continuously.

Increased specialization within disciplines; lack of meaningful interaction among disciplines; lack of substantive dialogue between higher education and industry; and antiquated teaching, curriculum development, and assessment practices are some of the factors responsible for a critical shortfall in higher education. But regardless of where we believe the problems originate, we can hone our own pedagogical practice, helping students to achieve more significant learning experiences. The learning portfolio is one practical solution.

Early each semester, I ask students to describe in writing their most significant learning experiences. We discuss the experiences as a group and explore the factors that made the experiences so meaningful. Predictable patterns emerge from students' accounts: being thrown into a situation and having to deal with it; experiences that evoked strong emotions; achieving or failing to achieve something of great personal value; experiences that challenged deeply held assumptions and beliefs. Rarely do students select experiences from their traditional education (college classes, high school) as their most significant learning moments. We talk about why that might be the case, discuss the concept of significant learning, and brainstorm ways in which each student could, in the context of my course, create a significant learning experience.

The activity described above serves as a springboard for discussions about how best to conceptualize learning and education and what those familiar words might actually mean. We discuss the terms within the context of the students' most significant learning experiences and come up with several common themes, including the important lesson that learning is a process of action and reflection.

Finally, we distinguish significant from casual learning by noting that it is more than just an accumulation of facts. Significant learning makes a difference in an individual's behavior, in the course of action chosen in the future, in attitude and personality. Students are quick to point out their perception of the weaknesses of their formal educational experiences, and they sense that significant learning forms the foundation for enduring, transferable skills. Within the context of such discussions, the concept of the learning portfolio first emerges.

THE LEARNING PORTFOLIO: A WORK IN PROCESS

I encourage students to think about the fundamental purpose of learning and education and the shape that their own learning may take in their lives. Such reflections serve to segue into the nature and value of learning portfolios. The portfolio is a command center for charting students' growth and development, passions and interests, goals and accomplishments.

My students are undergraduates seeking a Bachelor of Interdisciplinary Studies (BIS) degree. They combine two (or more) specific disciplines or concentration areas to create a customized field of study. The BIS program stresses the nature and value of interdisciplinarity in academics and in the workplace and helps students integrate their diverse interests in meaningful ways. Portfolios are introduced in the first course of a four-course sequence that all BIS majors must complete. Throughout the BIS core sequence, every student is expected to maintain a portfolio of work in the program.

Students revisit the portfolio development process in the final course in the sequence. From a programmatic perspective, the purpose of the portfolio is to allow students to track their intellectual progress, to think about what they have learned in-depth, and to identify strengths and areas for improvement as they proceed through the BIS program (see Augsburg in Part II of this volume for another perspective on portfolios in the BIS program).

From an interdisciplinary vantage, application of new knowledge and skills outside of the classroom environment and the transfer of crucial skills across domains are critical indicators of interdisciplinary effectiveness. The portfolio is an important piece in accomplishing the objective. When discussing the portfolio project with students, I stress that they should be concerned more with the portfolio development process than with the actual end product. Importantly, students must realize that their portfolios are developmental tools, works in process, and that the number of artifacts is not what counts, but rather the ways in which the portfolio will be used as they proceed with their education and their lives.

Accordingly, I provide students with guidelines for how to structure their own portfolios. I purposefully maintain a level of ambiguity in the guidelines because I want students to ask questions, struggle with the process, and ultimately create a portfolio that they personally value. The following is an excerpt from the portfolio development guidelines in my syllabus for the first course in the BIS core sequence:

> Your portfolio will include at least three sections as follows:
>
> **Section 1: The Learning Log.** In this section you will document and experiment with your learning over this semester and throughout your progress in the program. Consider the following learning objectives as you decide on the specific content and format for this section:
>
> • To create your own vivid record of the concepts and ideas that are most meaningful to you. To define, reflect on, translate, and transform key concepts and ideas we are exploring into a framework or context of your choice
>
> • To build creatively on what you are learning in your concentration areas, integrating your own unique perspectives, experiences, and insights; to discover connec-

tions among the concepts and ideas you are learning that would not have emerged in any other way

- To allow you easily to access the important materials you have collected for subsequent reflection and future development; to provide a tangible record of your progress as a self-directed learner and thinker

Remember that this section of your portfolio will include key artifacts of your learning in the program and your own reflections, connections, and actions with respect to the artifacts you present. . . .

Section 2: Transferable Skills. In this section you will document and discuss the transferable skills that you believe are most important for you to develop and demonstrate with respect to your own academic and career goals. Consider the following learning objectives as you decide on the specific content and format for this section:

- To define and explicate the specific transferable skills that you believe are most important to develop

- To provide an opportunity to collect artifacts that can be used to demonstrate your progress and effectiveness with respect to each of your selected skill areas

This section in your portfolio will be devoted to identifying and demonstrating that you possess specific transferable skills. The exact layout of this section will depend on you; however, be sure the section clearly identifies your transferable skills and offers evidence or artifacts of those skills. . . . Some examples of transferable skills would be public speaking, writing, intercultural communication, problem solving, leadership, flexibility/adaptability, teamwork, and learning skills.

Section 3: Plan-Of-Action. The last required section of your portfolio is your developmental plan-of-action with personal and professional goals. . . . Consider the following learning objectives as you decide on the specific content and format for this section:

- To develop expertise in effective goal setting, project management, and self-regulation of performance

- To allow you to consider and clarify your future goals with respect to your academics, your career, and your personal life

- Through the academic program of study, to help you gain clarity on your best path to graduation, based on what you want to get out of the program

This section of your portfolio will be devoted to dreams, desires, goals, and ambitions. You will practice charting your progress toward goals that are worthwhile to you.

I provide additional details and ideas regarding the development of each section and samples of prior exceptional student work. I also include several in-class portfolio-based activities and review sessions throughout the semester, allowing students to share creative ideas and limiting procrastination.

THE CLASSROOM EXPERIENCE AND ALIGNMENT OF GOALS

The student's effectiveness in developing a quality portfolio is greatly enhanced if the course is structured to touch regularly on significant learning and the benefits of portfolio development. Curriculum and specific portfolio objectives should be closely aligned. Assignments throughout the term should allow students to track progress toward goals of the portfolio and provide significant bridging to the portfolio process. Such assignments motivate students to think about learning as a process, requiring them to think in new ways, to reflect and create their own associations, to come up with their own theories, to integrate.

WHAT I LEARNED: A STUDENT'S PERSPECTIVE

Following, with permission, is one student's representative reflections on the portfolio process a few months after completion of the course. The reflections reinforce two key points: First, the importance of integrating the learning portfolio into the curriculum, not just using it as an added assignment; and second, the importance of the portfolio as an action-oriented process that results in behavioral changes and new perspectives for students and professors alike.

For "The Learning Portfolio," by Nicole Johanna Schultz

What have I learned?

I believe that out of all the sections in my portfolio, the plan of action illustrated my most significant learning. The entire section allowed me to define where I am going in the final years of my education. I expanded on my résumé, and I plotted which courses I have already taken and which courses I still am required to take. This brought the end into view and allowed me to start looking towards my future.

What am I doing differently?

This portfolio was a considerable amount of work. . . . Until this portfolio, I never really thought about the future at all. I always dreamed about graduating and starting a business, yet I never really had a grasp on how to get there. This portfolio pointed me in the right direction. . . .

Struggles

There were a lot of those. . . . To have to think about your future and realize you're only a semester away is a real shocker. This assignment was very difficult in many ways. My first struggle was figuring out what the teacher wanted from this assignment. My second struggle was realizing that it did not matter what the teacher wanted from this assignment because this was for me. After getting past the table of contents, the information was all there but I needed to put it all together. I managed to get through it all, but then I came to the hardest part of the assignment: explaining why I arranged things the way I did.

How I have used my portfolio

It has now only been a semester since this assignment was given, and I have used my portfolio a few times. Once in a job interview and another when I had to sign up for classes (there is the usefulness of the plan-of-action again). I plan on using my portfolio in the future, either for my career decisions or just to track my skills and accomplishments over the years (or maybe even both).

CONCLUSION

I've learned that three factors seem to be associated with one's commitment to lifelong learning and the development of a learning portfolio. First, we must get in touch with our vision, unique interests and passions, deepest goals and desires and then experience how learning can help move us toward what is important and valuable to us. Second, we must develop the appropriate tool set of skills and abilities to ensure that learning will be lasting and meaningful. And third, we must develop a strong sense of efficacy and confidence in our ability to meet specific goals and realize our personal vision.

The learning portfolio—because it values crossing disciplinary boundaries and facilitates action and reflection—is an effective process for developing such aims of lifelong learning. It is the most effective continuous personal improvement tool that I know.

The General Education Portfolio at Stephens College

Catherine M. Wehlburg
Texas Christian University

Stephens College is a small, four-year, private women's college. The goals of the general education program reflect, to a certain extent, the college's mission regarding women's scholarship and the education of women students. In addition, the general education program is a distribution type of program that contains both lower-division (freshman and sophomore level) and upper-division (junior and senior level) course requirements.

Stephens College has been actively assessing student learning outcomes using portfolio assessment since 1997. The portfolio that the student completes and submits is used to help faculty make curricular decisions about the content and sequencing of our general education program and to gather information (both quantitative and qualitative) concerning the actual learning outcomes shown by students.

Assessment using the General Education Portfolio is based on four principles:

1) The assessment should be a product of faculty and students together to discover information about student learning.

2) The resulting data should give information about the educational process that will result in increased student learning as measured by the stated general education outcomes.

3) The portfolio process will be folded into the ongoing life of the campus community and will involve faculty advisors and students.

4) Students will benefit from the portfolio process by gaining information about themselves and their relationship to the general education program.

Using this concept, the assessment process becomes one in which the student can gain information about learning at various points in the educational process. Even more importantly, individual faculty members within the institution can use the resulting data to make substantive and (relatively) immediate changes in course design, course sequencing, and the learning outcomes that are measured. Such efforts can lead to students and graduates who are more informed about general education and have a stronger learning base.

PROCESS FOR COMMUNICATING INFORMATION ON THE GENERAL EDUCATION PORTFOLIO

During the orientation period, incoming freshmen are required to attend several meetings and workshops. One of these involves the sharing of the portfolio process to be used in general education. Students are made aware that submitting the General Education Portfolio is a graduation requirement; if the portfolio is not submitted, the student's diploma will be held until the requirement is fulfilled. In addition, students are given the "General Education Portfolio Information" brochure that outlines the elements of the portfolio and has suggestions for saving course documents.

Elements of the General Education Portfolio

- Cover letter written by the student which describes the method used to put the portfolio together and what the student indicates was learned from the general education sequence at Stephens College

- Two documents/artifacts that show the student's growth as a critical thinker. One is from a course taken during the freshman or sophomore year and one from a course taken during the junior or senior year

- One document/artifact that shows the student's interdisciplinary thinking

- One document/artifact that shows student knowledge concerning women's issues and/or scholarship by and about women

- One document/artifact that shows student knowledge of cross-cultural issues related to the scholarship by ethnic minorities

- One document/artifact that shows the student's skills in using the scientific method or scientific reasoning

- One document/artifact that shows the student's skills in aesthetic analysis

- One document/artifact that the student considers to be one of the most personally satisfying experiences while at Stephens College

- The Writing Assessment Portfolio that is completed during the student's freshman year as she takes the required English sequence

Students are informed that they are expected to be reflective about their learning and that such reflection will enhance their undergraduate experience.

Students are also assured that the information gathered via the portfolio is not used in a punitive way. The brochure states:

> Stephens College is involved in actively assessing our education process to ensure that our students are given the best education possible. The faculty, administration, and staff are committed to maintaining our high academic standards and continuously improving the workings of our campus. In order to do this, we need to collect information from you, our first-year students, to help us in this task.
>
> We use portfolio assessment in order to help us make appropriate decisions about our general education programs. You will be collecting information that will eventually become a part of your general education portfolio (GEP). We will collect the GEP from you as you graduate.

Students are told that they will be working with their faculty advisors over the next four years to collect appropriate documents or artifacts. Students are assured that the GEP will not keep them from graduating, provided that the GEP is submitted by the required date. Faculty at Stephens College hope that such stipulations will allow students the freedom to be as critical about the program as necessary without fear of reprisal.

Letters are sent to graduating seniors in August and January, reminding them of the requirement to submit the GEP. In addition, faculty advisors are reminded to continue discussing the portfolio with students. We have found that simply by our asking faculty advisors to discuss the stated learning outcomes with students, faculty are making some changes in the general education courses that they teach. For example, syllabi are showing more direct referencing to the general education goal(s) for individual courses.

Along with the letters of reminder, graduating seniors receive a packet of individual cover sheets for each element of the portfolio. The cover sheets are filled out by the graduating senior, indicating how the chosen document demonstrates the required knowledge and/or skill. The cover sheet also asks the student to indicate how the institution might have helped the student improve in a particular area. For example, here are the questions for the "Interdisciplinary Thinking" element:

- Describe how this element displays interdisciplinary thinking.

- What could the college have done to help you improve in this area?

Faculty did not want students to spend hours putting the portfolio together, so the questions are very basic. However, when read by faculty, the portfolio usually reveals clearly when a student is not able to demonstrate knowledge of the area by the way she responds to such questions. The questions are also designed to help the student in her discussions with her advisor. The faculty believe that when a student knows the learning outcomes for general education, she will be more likely to look for the outcomes and will use them to see the overall importance of general education. In the past, some students (and faculty) have seen the general education sequence as merely a series of requirements/courses or hoops rather than a well-planned, meaningful series of courses that lead to the student's educational development and to the overall understanding of major intellectual issues.

Scoring and Using the Information

All of the GEPs are submitted to the office of the associate vice president for academic affairs. As students bring their portfolios to the office, their names are removed from the list. Students who do not submit the portfolio by the required date are sent an additional letter informing them that they have not turned in the portfolio and that it is a graduation requirement. Faculty advisors are also informed when one of their advisees has not submitted the GEP. With these steps, the return rate for GEPs has been over 95% for the last two years.

Following graduation, each portfolio is divided into its elements. For example, all of the "Aesthetic Analysis" sections of the portfolios are put together and all of the "Scientific Reasoning" sections are put together. No one person will ever read any individual student's portfolio because the faculty are not interested in how any one student performs; faculty are interested in how the graduating class as a whole performs on each element of the portfolio. The assessment process is focused on the institution's ability to provide for students the opportunity to show knowledge in the areas within general education. If many students show a lack of appropriate documentation of knowledge in any given element, faculty should look to the curriculum.

A faculty committee reads the elements of the portfolio. Most recently, that task has been given to the college-wide curriculum committee. Each faculty member on the committee reads all student submissions for one element. The faculty member scores each submission using a simple rubric. The aggregate data for each element is then submitted to the entire committee. The information is then shared with the full faculty. Discussions on curriculum can then occur on department and institutional levels.

Having the student actively think about the meaning of individual requirements and then discuss them with her advisor means that the student often is able to see the general education program as more than individual courses. And the student is then required to put all of the elements together and write a cover letter that encompasses the elements. Faculty hope that by using such a reflective method students will better understand the general education process and its importance. The data created by students are then used to inform the curricular decisions of faculty. The GEP process is an educational opportunity in which everybody wins—current students, faculty, and future students—a verification of the value of portfolio development for improvement and assessment of general education at Stephens College.

Part III

Sample Learning Portfolio Selections

The following section includes practical models and materials that suggest a variety of ways in which learning portfolios can be adapted across disciplinary courses, programs, and institutions. Some of the materials are print-based, some electronic, but the reader is encouraged to find creative ways of finding and applying common ideas and practices in the shared models and resources. The practical and highly adaptable examples of portfolio selections, assignments, guidelines, criteria, evaluation rubrics, and other resources are described below. In each case, sample portions of the student's portfolios are included rather than the entire document.

Robyn Allen, Wake Forest University. Master's, Biology Education. Demonstrates the usefulness of web-based portfolios in prompting students' reflection on the skills they learn and how best to communicate their learning against stated competencies and standards, including technology.

Dana L. Bennazar, University of North Florida. Education. An indication of the potentials inherent in electronic CD-ROM media for portfolio development.

Erin Claxton, University of North Florida. Education. Reveals the power of hyperlinks in electronic CD-ROM portfolios to help students tie reflections to multiple sources of evidence of their learning and pre-service skills.

Annette Collins, University of North Florida. Education. Provides an example of how LinkWay Live multimedia electronic portfolios allow student teachers to include multiple links to samples of their students' work and the outcomes of their learning in an elementary school classroom.

Alicia I. Gilbert, Arizona State University. Anthropology/Latin American Studies. Includes reflections on educational history and progress and a reflective analysis of academic and career values.

Emily Orser, Wake Forest University. Master's, English Education. Offers an example of how students can use digital portfolio technology to reflect on and organize the process and products of learning and develop a philosophy statement that provides a coherent framework for learning.

Lindsay Perani, University of North Florida. Education. Shows the value of an electronic PowerPoint portfolio in providing a teacher education student with an effective means of offering multisourced evidence of personal accomplishments and student outcomes in an internship.

Patrick Rickelton, Wake Forest University. Master's, Social Studies Education. Shares samples of electronic portfolio reflective statements tied to standards-based learning competencies and value of technology in learning.

Paul Rosenberg, Arizona State University. Business/Communication. An excerpt from the student's autobiographical reflections about educational background and goals, placing values and ambitions into reflective context.

Aryana Rousseau, Dalhousie University. Performing Arts, Communication, and Writing. Shares a student's reflection on the purpose of career portfolio development and its impact on educational goals.

Christina Teel, Arizona State University. Business/Communication. Develops an extensive, detailed list of skills learned in academic courses and other experiences and adds a reflective narrative to help organize and make educational and personal sense of the checklist.

Connie Thackaberry, Kent State University. Drama. Reviews the student's development through four years of college as an English major who became increasingly engaged with literature and with drama and acting.

Josee Vaillant, Dalhousie University. Education. Offers an example of a student's reflections on the purpose and value of the career portfolio process.

Jennifer Wolf, Albion College. Biology (pre-medicine). Demonstrates how the digital portfolio helps students document academic and other accomplishments and record, assess, and plan curricular progress, lending coherence and context to their learning.

ROBYN'S EDUCATION TECHNOLOGY WEBSITE

Hi. My name is Robyn Allen, and I would like to welcome you to this site that explores my experiences with technology in the Master Teacher Fellow Program at Wake Forest University. This year, I am preparing to become a Biology teacher at the secondary level. This particular career has been a dream of mine since my junior year of high school, and it is very exciting for me to watch it come true. This web site will contain my technology portfolio, which is not only required for licensure in North Carolina but will also teach me many areas of pedagogy and technology. People who might be interested in this site are other future teachers who want to view a technology portfolio, members of the Licensure Committee, and friends and family.

Components of My Technology Portfolio

Standards Newsletter

Field Trip Planning

Professional Presentation

Instructional Design Project

Technology Philosophy

Resources

North Carolina and National Educational Technology Standards

Some aspects of this portfolio will need Acrobat Reader software to view. Click here to download Acrobat Reader: http://www.adobe.com/products/acrobat/alternate.html#50

Personally . . .

I am a graduate from the "university of the people," UNC at Chapel Hill. (GO HEELS!!!!) As a "born" and "bred" Tar Heel, I am finding life at another ACC school difficult. Not academically of course, but more along the lines of when is it appropriate to wear a Carolina Blue T-shirt without getting mobbed by a jealous crowd (just kidding, to my WFU friends). Needless to say I love watching sports, especially my Heels, but I also enjoy reading, watching movies, and being outside and enjoying nature. My newest and favorite love, though, is my husband, Rodney.

Together we are forming the other important aspect of my life-family. My parents, brothers, and now Rodney have kept me grounded (with sarcasm

The interaction of animals and plants drives the cycle of nature.	The birth of new life reveals the wonder of genetics and evolution.	Habitats like this coral reef are important areas of biodiversity on our planet.	Raptors, like this bald eagle, are at the top of the food chain.	Plants are the beginning of life due to food and oxygen production.

mostly), which will hopefully help me in the classroom.

I hope that you enjoy your stay and will return soon! Get out there and enjoy SCIENCE!!!

Contact me at allerj1@wfu.edu
This website was last updated February 10, 2002.

REFLECTION ON THE CREATION OF MY STANDARDS NEWSLETTER

View the Competencies Covered by This Project

In preparing the Standards Newsletter, I was able to see and to understand the skills necessary in publishing something for parents. Before this task, I assumed that things of this nature were relatively easy, but now I realize the time and energy that using the Publisher software requires. Once I knew it a little better, I was able to manipulate text and picture with greater ease, but it was still time consuming. This exercise showed me that when producing an involved newsletter or other letter to go home, much thought and preparation must be put into it. For instance, I had to know the Technology standards for both teachers and students as well as the Biology standards so that I could express to parents the way that science teachers were going to integrate technology into the Biology curriculum. To find out about each of the standards required for both students and teachers, I went to the NC Department of Education web site to find requirements for both groups and content areas. The National

Education Technology Standards for students and teachers was at the web site for the International Society for Technology in Education.

I also learned to think about who my readers were going to be. Parents need to know that teachers are going to do everything to help their students succeed, so I included information such as class technology activities, projects that are new additions to the curriculum, technology training of teachers, and their child's use of computers while at school (availability times in and out of class so that no parent thought they would have to buy a computer for the home).

Another aspect of parent communication is readability and attractiveness. One would hope that all parents would automatically read any papers sent home but sometimes this does not happen. To combat this, I included graphics to the newsletter, as well as different colored fonts to give the reader something to look at besides words. These pictures and textboxes also sum up the given information so the parent can know immediately what he or she is about to read. I also worked on picking a font that was easy to read and tried to make my language easy to understand and as narrative as possible. I wanted my parents to get the needed information quickly with as little effort as possible. Any correspondence with parents should not be preachy or too erudite in order not to offend; teachers and parents must work together to ensure a quality education. Any publication to students or parents, such as a syllabus, newsletter, conference request, discipline notice, or positive announcement, should be as professional as possible with aspects that show your creative and caring sides as well.

I believe that the Microsoft Publisher software is a useful tool for producing documents within the classroom setting. From awards to calendars, a teacher has so many wonderful options at his or her fingertips. I am lucky enough to have this on my personal computer, but if it is not included at a school site, a teacher could be missing out on one the easiest ways to create paper products that are great supplements to any classroom environment. The communication aspect is probably where it is most important, especially for items like newsletters to parents, calendars for a class or club, and letterhead for professional letters. This program is also easily teachable to a class of students who could themselves use it for presentations on topics in Biology by using brochures, newsletters, web sites, or posters. With the proper preparation before starting, Publisher will be an excellent way for me to communicate with parents or students and will be an important way for me to teach my own students technology skills as I try and integrate computers in my content area.

COMPETENCIES COVERED BY THIS PROJECT

NC Competencies–Basic

3.1 Word Processing

3.2 Copy and move blocks of text

3.3 Change text format and style, set margin, line spacing, tabs

3.4 Check spelling, grammar, word usage

3.5 Create a header or footer

3.6 Insert date, time, page number

3.7 Add columns to document

3.8 Insert clip art into document

8.1 Produce print-based products

8.6 Role of media in effective communication

NC Competencies–Advanced

10.1 Use Computer Skills Curriculum

12.3 Use computers to communicate effectively

NETS

I. Technology operations and concepts–A and B

II. Planning and designing learning environments
and experiences–A

III. Teaching, learning, and the curriculum–A

IV. Productivity and professional practice–B, C, and D

View My Standards Newsletter as a PDF

TECHNOLOGY PHILOSOPHY

Learning to use technology effectively has given me many options for teaching opportunities as well as chances to improve my personal productivity. With only training in word processing and the Internet, I knew that my skills were insufficient to not only use technology for learning but also to teach tech skills to my students. This class has provided me with the knowledge to both use and teach many programs in my classroom.

With so many things for a teacher to do, it is necessary to find ways to easily do large tasks. Communicating with parents becomes quick and easy, yet very professional, with mail merge options within software. Also, Publishing software allows me to create powerful newsletters for parents. Students can use this program to make productions for projects to show what they have learned. Creating lessons, notes, and concept maps are simple with word processing programs and other software such as Inspiration. These can be saved and used year after year as well as have changes made easily to them upon reflection of the lesson. These programs are also easy for students to learn how to use as production tools. Programs like Inspiration also provide methods to make ideas visible; visualization is a way to reach all learners with one lesson aspect. Using these many programs also allows the teacher to use multiple methods of presenting content, such as pictures, written instructions, etc.

It is important also to remember that teaching technology must be coupled with lessons concerning Internet safety and copyright issues. Students must be taught by both example and instruction from myself how to use the Internet to gain the information they need or want without exposing themselves to the questionable people and websites that exist today. Though most schools will participate in filtering programs, I believe that an education program is much more important and effective to teach students the proper way to use technology. This program should also include in-depth information concerning copyright information so that students will understand its implications and repercussions. In dealing with access for all students, it is necessary to be supported by an administration who believes in spending money on technology for all classrooms and labs so students can get lots of experience both in and out of the classroom.

I look forward to using technology to help teach all students in my classroom to the best of my ability. Technology offers so many more options for teachers to try and reach all learning types than ever before. It also assists teachers in presenting many key aspects in learning science such as problem solving and analysis. Programs and software also make most lesson plans more intricate with less work if proper training and practice is employed. I feel that my training has given me the start that I need to use technology in my classroom both for my students and myself.

Return to the Top of the Page
    Home Page
    Standards Newsletter
    Field Trip Planning
    Professional Presentation
    Instructional Design Project
    Technology Philosophy
    Resources
    NC and NETS Technology Standards

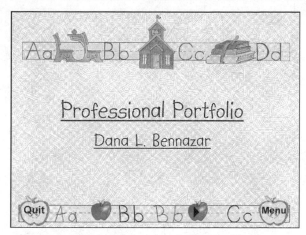

Professional Portfolio
Dana L. Bennazar

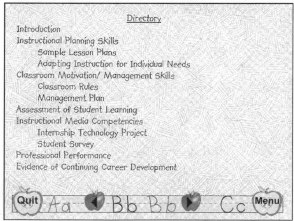

Directory

Introduction
Instructional Planning Skills
    Sample Lesson Plans
    Adapting Instruction for Individual Needs
Classroom Motivation/ Management Skills
    Classroom Rules
    Management Plan
Assessment of Student Learning
Instructional Media Competencies
    Internship Technology Project
    Student Survey
Professional Performance
Evidence of Continuing Career Development

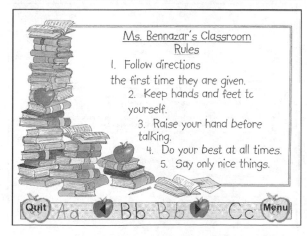

Ms. Bennazar's Classroom Rules

1. Follow directions the first time they are given.
2. Keep hands and feet to yourself.
3. Raise your hand before talking.
4. Do your best at all times.
5. Say only nice things.

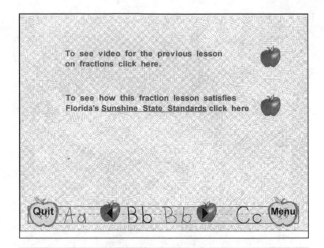

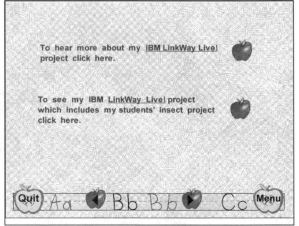

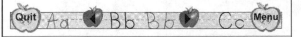

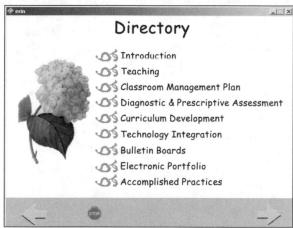

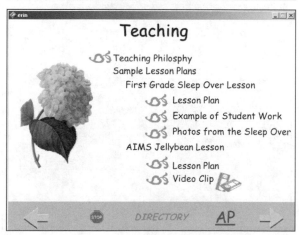

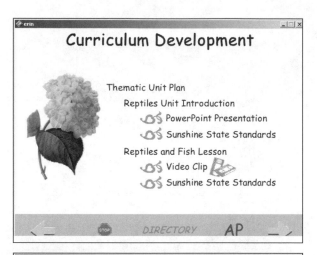

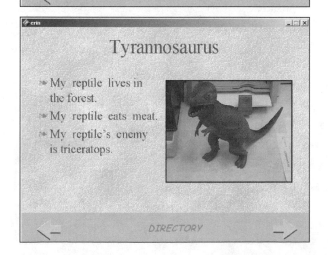

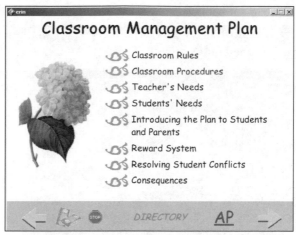

Classroom Management Plan

- Classroom Rules
- Classroom Procedures
- Teacher's Needs
- Students' Needs
- Introducing the Plan to Students and Parents
- Reward System
- Resolving Student Conflicts
- Consequences

DIRECTORY   AP

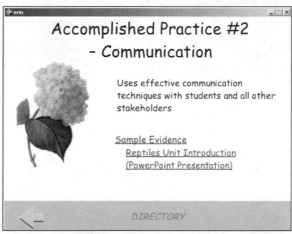

Accomplished Practice #2 – Communication

Uses effective communication techniques with students and all other stakeholders

Sample Evidence
Reptiles Unit Introduction
(PowerPoint Presentation)

DIRECTORY

Reptiles

snakes   turtles   alligators

lizards   crocodiles

DIRECTORY

ANNETTE COLLINS'S ELECTRONIC PORTFOLIO

The following are illustrations from the LinkWay Live folder of Annette Collins. (Year 5 of the Lone Star 2000 Project).

Illustration 1 above

This is the first slide of Annette's electronic portfolio showing her picture and a brief description of what the viewers will be seeing in the presentation.

Illustration 2 below

This slide shows the creative way Annette divided her students into groups and the manner in which she guided the viewer to the samples of their work.

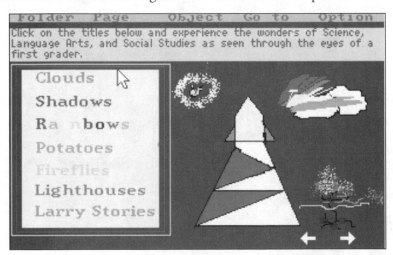

Illustration 3 above

This slide is an example from the "Cloud" group. The student did both the drawing and the writing.

Illustration 4 below

This slide is an example from the "Shadow" group. The child demonstrates his knowledge of the science subject matter.

Illustration 5 above

This is an example from the "Rainbow" group. Each student chose his or her own background and colors for the slide.

Illustration 6 below

This is an example from the "Fireflies" group. Knowledge of the science subject matter is evident in the text.

Illustration 7 above

This is an example from the "Lighthouse" group. This student demonstrated a remarkable ability to illustrate the subject and condense the most important information into a single slide

Illustration 8 below

This is an example from the "Larry Stories" group. The child created an original story and illustrated it appropriately.

ALICIA I. GILBERT
Learning Portfolio
BIS 301, Spring 2001
Arizona State University

TABLE OF CONTENTS

17) BIS résumé

18) Advertisements from graduate student forum of The Society for Latin American Anthropology

19) My path to my dream job

FINDING A CACTUS FLOWER: MY EDUCATIONAL JOURNEY
(BIS Autobiography)

When I began my collegiate career, I had a murky perception of what I wanted to do in my adulthood. Because I am the granddaughter of a pastor and civil rights advocate, my maturation occurred in the public eye. Although I tried constantly to resist it, people seemed fascinated with my family's life. Until this point, the careful guides of my family and church had molded all of my experiences.

Before my high school years, the only career I wanted was in the arts. During my childhood, everything I did led me in this direction. I was a singer, a musician, a dancer, and an actress. I did some typical childhood activities such as school plays, choir, band. However, I also did some atypical activities: songwriting, playwriting, and broadcasting. Until I was about 14, I never imagined any other way of life.

Doubt set in when I was about 14 because my mother discovered something: my journal. I had been writing since I was about 11. I kept a journal that had diary entries in it, but it also included my sketches, songs, and some of my other work. My mother had been in my room and had discovered it. It must have taken her a couple of hours to look through it and to read everything in it.

Then, she did the unthinkable: She wrote a lengthy response in it. I thought I had safely concealed some of my doubts and fears in that journal—the main one being that I had no other career ideas for my life. One of the statements she wrote was, "You seem to be a good reporter, and you should try journalism."

She had a point. I had been writing for school, church, and community newspapers for a long time. It was something that I enjoyed doing. However, my mother also wrote that I was wasting my time thinking that I could have a career in the arts. I recall her stating that musicians usually end up using drugs and that she did not expect me to have such a life.

So my participation in the arts slowly decreased, and my intrigue in journalism increased. By 1989, I was graduating in the top of my class. I had many college scholarship offers, even one to West Point, but I am an

Air Force brat, and I didn't want to be in the military at any level. This was completely against my family's wishes. People from the church thought I had lost my mind. A good family friend recommended that we tour Western Kentucky University. She is an alumna, and she offered to go with us on the tour.

Because of the tour, I found myself on Western Kentucky University's campus in August 1989, away from all I had known for the first time in my life. The overachieving, people-pleasing little girl was terrified of failure.

For me, failure meant attending college for four years, graduating, and working a job instead of having a career. Somehow, I lost the will to be the best journalist that I could be during my junior year. I was under pressure to choose a minor. There were many subjects that I was interested in, but I still felt I had to meet my family's approval. After all, they were helping me pay some of my college expenses. Although I had taken classes in French, Portuguese, and Spanish, I felt that I could not choose any of these as a minor. I enjoyed studying these languages, but I was living in the south and had little opportunity to improve my skills. Also, I am an Arizona native who first learned to speak Spanish as a child while playing with Spanish-speaking children. When we moved to Tennessee, I lost the ability to speak Spanish. In other words, I did not have the confidence during my time at Western to choose a language as a minor.

Although I continued to take ballet classes, I felt that my dancing wasn't as good after a foot injury during my sophomore year. I had to consider the personal struggles a professional dancer experiences. I had witnessed what friends of mine were going through in that world. I decided that I would not minor in dance.

At that time I had thought about anthropology, but I was honestly worried about my family's opinion. Worse, what would the church think about this? Once again, I decided not to minor in anthropology.

My ballet professor's ex-husband was the head of the theater department, and I decided to go talk to him. I wanted to know what his thoughts were about a journalism and theater combination for my studies. He thought it was an interesting idea. Therefore, I pursued theater as my minor, without my family's knowledge until a few months before graduation. I began to study languages more and I also began to study Latin America. In reality, my interdisciplinary studies began about ten years ago. My last two years at Western were an improvement over the first two. Although I graduated quite high in my class, I felt like a failure. I had a journalism degree, yet I was not looking forward to working in news.

Before venturing off to work, I was going to attend graduate school in England. During this time, I fell in love. We were supposed to get married. When the relationship broke up, I stayed in the States. I was not able to find the kind of journalism job that I wanted. After only a few months in the field, I decided that journalism was not for me.

My undergraduate studies at Western were not entirely in vain. The university's motto is "The Spirit Makes the Master." Now that I am an alumna, I realize how true that statement is. During my time there, I had a poor spirit. I had no idea how to take risks. At the time, I was too cowardly to stand up for my convictions.

After I cancelled my study-abroad plans, my parents decided to move back to Arizona. At the time, my mother had been working for Sprint for five years. Sprint's center in Nashville closed unexpectedly. She was offered the chance to transfer. She asked me if I wanted to move to Arizona with them. One thing that I had wanted to do for a long time was to return to Arizona. I missed living in the Southwest. I felt that this was a chance for me to have a more normal life. I decided to move to Arizona.

In September 1994, I moved back to Arizona. My plan was to move to Arizona and to attend Arizona State University the following year. About three months after I moved back, my paternal grandmother died suddenly. Her death was the first event that made me think about my own life. Because of her death, I changed jobs. I worked in public relations for a brief time, but I knew it was not what I should be doing. I wanted to learn more about Latin America, and I wanted to improve my ability to speak Spanish. In November 1995, I began working at Sprint. Because I work at Sprint's International Dialing Center, I've known people from numerous cultures. I've learned more not only about Latin Americans, but also about how well diversity can work in a company.

The second event was the theft of my identity by someone I know very well. I found out about it in December 1997. My journalism skills helped me greatly during that ordeal because I was able to find out who used my information to make purchases with it. It was a difficult time for me. However, after this happened to me, I became more focused on how I wanted my life to change. I worked diligently for two years on discovering who I really am. When someone takes your identity, the theft makes you question what makes you *you*.

The third event that happened to me was early in 1999. A childhood friend was gunned down in his own home. We were a year apart in age. Because this happened to someone I had known for over 20 years, I was more determined than ever that my life would not be in vain. I specifically remember that two weeks after his death, I honored his memory by going to Arizona State University and getting all the information I could about communications, anthropology, and Latin American studies. I applied to ASU's undergraduate and graduate programs. I had no idea how I was going to do it, but I was determined to return to an academic life for awhile because that is where I belong.

Although it would be easy just to get a master's degree and go on with my life, I found out that I could earn another bachelor's degree fairly quickly. I decided to do this because the Interdisciplinary Studies programs at ASU appealed to me as a path leading me to a combination of areas. Reading Gary Zukav's *Seat of the Soul* also made my decision easier. Once I discovered that I needed "to align all of my other ships with my Mother Ship," I knew that I must stop conforming to what others wanted me to do. I began to stand up for my own convictions. It was simply time for me to be myself. If my family and my church could not understand, then I felt the failure was their problem. At 28, I decided that I would not think of others this time. I would think of myself and do what felt right.

To study anthropology and Latin American studies is a natural part of my life. Anthropology is the one area in which I can explore *all* of the things I've ever been interested in. I can do work in this field and not feel like it's work. Confucius said that if you do what you love, you'll never work again. I've always had a love for Latin American culture. I am of Latin American descent (Haitian), so I suppose my attraction is natural. In the past couple of years I've realized that language and culture have always captivated my attention. When I was heavily participating in the arts, I was participating in culture. Recently, a friend of mine has helped me to realize how interested I am in religion. I've always been interested in the role religion has in our lives. Just last year I wrote a paper about the religious restraints on our appearance. I'm interested in not just Christianity, but other religions, too. By attending ASU, I've been exposed to many religions. I've learned more about Islam, Judaism, The Ba'hai, Voodoo, Santeria, and countless others.

I am not just an interdisciplinary studies student now. I have an interdisciplinary *life*.

REFLECTION ON VALUES CHECKLIST

A career as a cultural anthropologist matches well with my core work values. Both of my concentration areas utilize the values that are significantly important to me. I am able to work on long-term projects, work independently, work with ideas, work with people, and work with a flexible schedule.

Because I enjoy doing extensive research, I am able to work on long-term projects. I enjoy visiting libraries, visiting newspaper morgues, researching online, and interviewing people. All of these activities are vital to doing extensive research. One of my goals is to do research during my academic career. However, I would also enjoy a research job in the field of cultural anthropology. A dream come true for me would be to do extensive research in Latino communities in the United States. One idea I have is to research the impact that the "English for the Children" propositions will have on non-English-proficient Latino public school children in the Southwest. Another is to research organized religion's restrictions on appearance. I have researched both topics before, but the research was marginal. The kind of research I want to do will take years. Even if I do not have a career that allows me to do such research, I intend to continue it on my own.

Often one must work independently when doing a long-term project. Cultural anthropology is conducive to such work. When anthropologists write an ethnography, often they work alone to collect and organize data. I do not require constant supervision, so cultural anthropology would be a good career, allowing considerable autonomy to gather data.

Because I have a background in print journalism, creative writing, and fine arts, I enjoy working with ideas. The ideas do not have to be my own. If I am doing teamwork and someone else on the team has an idea, then I will collaborate with that person. In the end, each person should receive credit for his or her contributions to the work. Ideas are essential to cultural anthropologists because they are a starting point for meaningful research.

A cultural anthropologist must have a flexible schedule. Often the anthropologist must arrange his or her schedule according to when informants are available. Also, some cultural events are unexpected, not neatly scheduled. A cultural anthropologist can study how people in a particular group respond to such events.

Such basic values complement my ambition to be a cultural anthropologist. The basic values may also work well in other careers, but I cannot imagine myself doing anything else at this point in my life.

EMILY ORSER'S
SUPER SNAZZY EDUCATION HOMEPAGE

Welcome to my very first web site!

I am a Master Teacher Fellow in the Department of Education at Wake Forest University studying to become a high school English teacher. I hope that those of you who visit this page—students, parents, teachers, and friends—will find out a little more about me, my background and aspirations, as well as links to my Technology Portfolio, a North Carolina licensure requirement that I created in my Technology in Education class.

On this site...
A little about me...
e-mail me!
"Just" a teacher?
Standards Newsletter
National and NC Standards Correlations
Planning a Field Experience
Web Safety, Access, and Official Use
Instructional Design Project
My Technology Philosophy
Resources

A little about me...

Born in Boston, my family and I moved from Wellesley, Massachusetts, to North Carolina when I was ten years old and have been here ever since. Although I am a Yankee, "y'all" now has a permanent place in my vocabulary. I went to public school until the ninth grade, when I attended Salem Academy, a school for young women.

From Salem, I went to Wake Forest to study English and music. In the spring of my junior year I studied abroad in Vienna. My main interest, as far as my academic studies goes, has concentrated on women's works, both literary and musical. Last fall, I completed a research project on women's music and performed a Senior Voice Recital to share what I had learned throughout my two years of research and practice. It was an amazing experience to sing for an audience of five hundred. Two weeks after my graduation, I began the Master Teacher Fellows Program at Wake and am concentrating on learning as much as I can about students, teaching, and myself so that I can become the best English teacher I can be.

e-mail me!
I welcome your suggestions, questions, and concerns. My address is emily orser@alumni.wfu.edu

"Just" a teacher?
Many people have asked me recently if I am going to be "just" a teacher, and I would like to take a second to respond. Even at its most literal level, no teacher is "just" a teacher. Teachers are also counselors, role models, muses, performers, and artists. Teaching should never be preceded by "just"; my teachers have been the noblest people I have ever known, precisely because they are so underpaid and under-appreciated.

But before you think that I am getting too negative, teaching also provides the greatest opportunity to give back to others and our communities what we have been given. Of course, I have to admit that being "noble" is not what I am after—I love English, I love high school students, and I love learning; I want to be challenged, and most of all, I need to feel that my job has a purpose, which, for me, turns out to be teaching. That is why I want to teach.

You will need Adobe Acrobat to read some documents in this site. If you do not have the Acrobat Reader, you can download it with the above link for free.

INSTRUCTIONAL DESIGN UNIT

The creation of this Instructional Design Unit has allowed me to consider many aspects of unit planning and technology integration as important to teaching and student learning. Careful attention to content, state and national standards, and student learner aptitude and diverse needs are among the primary considerations.

It is vital that content meet both curricular and technology standards in as many ways as possible. When curricular standards drive a unit, content can be overlooked in favor of "covering" the lists. On the other hand, when content and curricular standards are considered together, the unit allows students to integrate their knowledge and competencies with state and national expectations. Technology standards should also be well integrated with content. It is an understatement that teachers must be competent with basic technology processes and applications in order to serve as technology educators for students. For students, knowing and having experience with technology is vital to their academic and professional success. Although many students are well beyond their teachers' capabilities, many others have limited or no access to technology outside school and it is up to educators to help those students develop competence and introduce new and alternative technologies to all. In this unit, the concept mapping with Inspiration creates a venue for students to work with a software that is likely unfamiliar and produce tools for their own learning and understanding. The "Film Friezes" component allows students to use digital cameras hands-on, a technology with which many students may be unfamiliar, and communicate their ideas through the PowerPoint presentation.

I hope you will enjoy exploring the process and products of this project:
> Cover Page
> Author Information
> Overview
> Learner Description
> Procedures and Products
> Products:
> Character Concept Mapping
> The Female Bildungsroman PowerPoint
> Fried Green Tomatoes DVD Clips
> Film Directors PowerPoint
> Resources
> Assessment Strategy and Rubric
> Universal Design for Learning Analysis

NORTH CAROLINA AND NATIONAL TECHNOLOGY STANDARDS
MET BY THIS PROJECT: NORTH CAROLINA BASIC & ADVANCED TECHNOLOGY STANDARDS FOR TEACHERS:

> 1.0 Computer Operation Skills

Essential Knowledge and Skills:
1.1 Start up and shut down computer system and peripherals
1.2 Identify and use icons, windows, menus
1.3 Start an application and create a document
1.4 Name, save, retrieve, revise a document
1.5 Use printing options
1.6 Insert and eject floppy disk and CD-ROM
1.7 Initialize, name/rename floppy disk and hard disk
1.8 Copy document from hard disk to floppy disk and vice versa
1.9 Create and name/rename subdirectories/folders
1.10 Save, open, place documents inside subdirectories/folders
1.11 Open and work with more than one application at a time

2.0 Setup, Maintenance, and Troubleshooting
Essential Knowledge and Skills:
2.4 Make backup copies of key applications and documents
2.5 Use self-help resources to diagnose and correct common hard-ware/printing problems

3.0 Word Processing/Introductory Desktop Publishing
Essential Knowledge and Skills:
3.1 Enter and edit text and copy and move a block of text
3.2 Copy and move blocks of text
3.3 Change text format and style, set margin, line spacing, tabs
3.4 Check spelling, grammar, word usage
3.8 Insert clip art into document

6.0 Networking
Essential Knowledge and Skills:
6.1 Use a file server (connect/log on, retrieve a program or document, save a document to a specified location)

7.0 Telecommunications
Essential Knowledge and Skills:
7.1 Connect to the Internet or an on-line service
7.3 Access and use resources on Internet and World Wide Web

8.0 Media Communications (including image and audio processing)
Essential Knowledge and Skills:
8.3 Set up and operate a videocassette recorder/player and monitor/TV

8.4 Connect a video output device (e.g., LCD panel) to computer for large screen display

Expanded Knowledge and Skills:

8.10 Use digital camera and scanner

8.13 Set up and operate a videodisk player and TV receiver or monitor

9.0 Multimedia Integration

Essential Knowledge and Skills:

9.1 Use a linear multimedia presentation

9.2 Use a non-linear, hypermedia presentation

Expanded Knowledge and Skills:

9.4 Plan/produce a linear multimedia presentation

9.5 Plan/produce a non-linear, hypermedia presentation

National Educational Technology Standards for Teachers:

I. Technology Operations and Concepts

Teachers demonstrate a sound understanding of technology operations and concepts. Teachers:

A. demonstrate introductory knowledge, skills, and understanding of concepts related to technology (as described in the ISTE National Education Technology Standards for Students).

B. demonstrate continual growth in technology knowledge and skills to stay abreast of current and emerging technologies.

II. Planning and Designing Learning Environments and Experiences

Teachers plan and design effective learning environments and experiences supported by technology. Teachers:

A. design developmentally appropriate learning opportunities that apply technology-enhanced instructional strategies to support the diverse needs of learners.

C. identify and locate technology resources and evaluate them for accuracy and suitability.

D. plan for the management of technology resources within the context of learning activities.

E. plan strategies to manage student learning in a technology-enhanced environment.

III. Teaching, Learning, and the Curriculum
Teachers implement curriculum plans, that include methods and strategies for applying technology to maximize student learning. Teachers:

A. facilitate technology-enhanced experiences that address content standards and student technology standards.

B. use technology to support learner-centered strategies that address the diverse needs of students

C apply technology to develop students' higher order skills and creativity.

D. manage student learning activities in a technology-enhanced environment.

IV. Assessment and Evaluation
Teachers apply technology to facilitate a variety of effective assessment and evaluation strategies. Teachers:

A. apply technology in assessing student learning of subject matter using a variety of assessment techniques.

C. apply multiple methods of evaluation to determine students' appropriate use of technology resources for learning, communication, and productivity.

V. Productivity and Professional Practice
Teachers use technology to enhance their productivity and professional practice. Teachers:

B. continually evaluate and reflect on professional practice to make informed decisions regarding the use of technology in support of student learning.

VI. Social, Ethical, Legal, and Human Issues
Teachers understand the social, ethical, legal, and human issues surrounding the use of technology in PK–12 schools and apply those principles in practice. Teachers:

A. model and teach legal and ethical practice related to technology use.

B. apply technology resources to enable and empower learners with diverse backgrounds, characteristics, and abilities.

C identify and use technology resources that affirm diversity.

D. promote safe and healthy use of technology resources.

E. facilitate equitable access to technology resources for all students.

MY TECHNOLOGY IN EDUCATION PHILOSOPHY

The way I regarded technology in education before I took this class was something akin to bigotry. Just as a person who feels prejudice for others often bases her generalizations on a few, often skewed, experiences, I often viewed the use of technology in the classroom as an impediment to learning. The few experiences I had in a few of my college courses seemed to teach me that technology was not only unnecessary, but a cumbersome waste of time. I thought that technology had no place in my English classroom. However, after experiencing many educational technologies firsthand, I am beginning, and hope to continue, to see their beneficial applications. Although I maintain that technology can never take the place of intelligent, passionate, and connected teaching, I realize that the skillful and effective use of technology supports, not replaces, good teachers and good teaching.

The benefits for personal productivity are extensive. Options like e-mail and mail merge, programs like Word and Access, as well as the Internet will be infinitely helpful in maintaining my personal and professional organization and sanity. I plan to use e-mail and mail merge (with Access) extensively to communicate with parents, students, and colleagues. This will not only facilitate collaboration, but will also allow me to communicate with more than one person at a time and address questions and concerns as they arise, whether they come during the work day or after-hours. By maintaining class memos and handouts in Word, I will be able make minor corrections on frequently used documents. The Internet is an inexhaustible and accessible resource of which I plan to make the most.

I intend that my students will take advantage of as many applicable technologies as possible, in an effort to ensure that students achieve technological proficiency. I hope that students will be able to work with computer technologies such as Word, Excel, Access, Publisher, Inspiration, Power-Point, the Internet, e-mail, and mail merge; communications technologies such as CD, CD-ROM, TV, VCR, Laserdisc, and DVD; and representational technologies like digital cameras and video. I expect both that students will become more proficient and technology-savvy with greater access and experience and that these technological supports will enhance their learning and incite them to further exploration. That said, I will require safe and ethical use of technologies from my students. I will communicate, support, and enforce the Acceptable Use Policy of my school with my students to ensure their safety and productivity. My classes and I will adhere to Fair Use guidelines and copyright law.

Although some students in the United States are not given equal access to technology, it is my responsibility that—at least in my classroom with whatever technologies are available—students are given equal access to computers and other technologies. This should also be true of the way information is expressed in class. I plan to adhere to the tenets of Universal Design in order to use students' multiple ways of learning as a guide which will improve all students' learning. By employing PowerPoint, CD-ROM, video, DVD, Laserdisc, multiple language tracks and subtitles, text reading and writing programs, and other multiple representations of content, students will have more opportunities to understand material and demonstrate their knowledge in ways that will improve learning.

Because I have had the opportunity to "meet" these diverse and exciting technologies personally, I have become familiar with technology's educational capability and potential. It is my impossible hope that I will be able to share all that I have learned in my students' education. I know that I will make use of as much as I can.

If you haven't already, you may want to check out the National and NC Standards Correlations page.

| Home | Standards Newsletter |
| National and NC Standards Correlations |
| Planning a Field Experience |
| Web Safety, Access, and Official Use |
| Instructional Design Project | Resources |

Ms. Lindsay Perani

Internship:
Lone Star Elementary School
Directing Teacher:
Ms. Marla Hamela

Table Of Contents:

 Teaching Philosophy

 Experiences with Children

 Classroom Management Plan

 Student Work

Teaching Philosophy

My classroom is an environment which fosters critical thinking, a positive self-image, responsibility, and an understanding that effort and cooperation will lead to success in preparing for tomorrow's world.

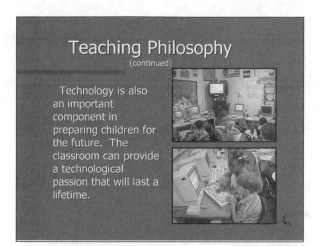

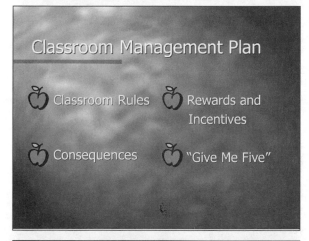

Rewards and Incentives

- Verbal Praise
- Stickers and Treats
- Phone Calls
- Fun Friday
- Lunch with Teacher

Student Work

 If You Give A _____ A _____...

 My Favorite Breakfast...

 My Cracked Egg...

 Our Sleepover...

If You Give A _____ A _____...

The idea for this writing lesson was inspired by author Laura Joffe Numeroff and her zany stories. During the week of March 8-12, we read her three books, "If You Give a Mouse a Cookie", "If You Give A Moose A Muffin", and "If You Give A Pig A Pancake". After that, we wrote a class story, individual stories, made mouse cookies, pancakes, and blueberry muffins.

"If You Give A Toucan A Taco..."
By: Our Class

If you give a toucan a taco, he will want some hot taco sauce to go with it. So, you will bring him some of your grandmother's homemade sauce. When he is finished eating the taco, he will want another, and another. When they are gone, you will have to go to Taco Bell to get some more...

"If You Give An Intern A Skillet..."
By: Miss Perani

If you give an intern a skillet, she will want some pancake batter to go with it. Once she gets the batter, she will want a spatula. After she makes the pancakes, she will want a hungry class to eat them.

My Favorite Breakfast...

George Shrinks, by William Joyce, was one of our favorite stories this year. In the story, George gets to eat whatever he wants for breakfast. We decided to write about our favorite breakfasts and illustrate them.

"Eggs, Grits, and Toast"
By: Hosea Cason

If I could eat anything for breakfast, it would be eggs, grits, and toast. They smell good. It tastes plain. It feels gushy. I like to mix my eggs and grits together.

Our Sleepover...

On February 26, six first grade classes at Lone Star had a sleepover from 11 - noon. Two stories, "A Great Place for Llama" and "Never Wake a Sleeping Snake" inspired us to have our sleepover. We also read to the Duval County School Board employees in our pajamas. This showed everyone that to reach our goal of reading 25 books, we read each night before going to bed.

Patrick Rickelton's
Technology in Education for Social Studies Website

Welcome. My name is Patrick Rickelton and this is my website devoted to technology in education. I am a Master Teacher Fellow in the Department of Education at Wake Forest University in Winston-Salem, NC. Having graduated in 1999 from Lipscomb University in Nashville, TN with a B.A. in History & German, I decided to disappear into the business world for a couple of years. All the while I was teaching ESL to anyone I met who needed it, and found it to be both exciting and worthwhile. This discovery has recently brought me to Wake Forest, where I am studying full-time on a fellowship. At the moment I am in the process of earning my license as a secondary social studies teacher.

The better part of this website is a technology portfolio. The following components have been created to demonstrate my ability to use technology to support teaching and learning:

- Standards Newsletter and Reflection

- Technology Standards

- Field Trip Planning and Reflection

- Professional Presentation and Reflection

- Instructional Design Project and Reflection

- My Technology Philosophy

- Resources

You probably assume that this portfolio is an undertaking conceived one Sunday afternoon on the porch with a glass of tea in hand, wondering what I could do with all of my free time. Surprisingly, that is not the case.

I have created this portfolio to show that I have met the North Carolina Department of Public Standards and the National Educational Technology Standards (as created by the International Society for Technology in Education). The technology portfolio is a requirement for anyone seeking an initial teacher's license in the state of North Carolina. In reality I am thankful for such a requirement, as it has increased my understanding and capabilities in the world of computers. I am anxious to put these newfound skills to use in the classroom to better accommodate a variety of learners and learning styles.

You will need Adobe Acrobat Reader to view some files. You can download a reader for free here.

Last updated January 28, 2002
Contact info: rickph1@wfu.edu

STANDARDS NEWSLETTER

In preparing the standards newsletter for parents, I was excited that for me the possibilities had multiplied. Prior to using Microsoft Publisher my only experience with design had been with word processors and spreadsheets, rather limited formats. But the seemingly endless choices of alterable templates provided by Publisher broadened my conception of what one can do with a simple PC. Concomitant with this was the realization that there is software for practically any application.

Beyond the ability to create a newsletter for parents, this technology can be used to serve me as a teacher in a myriad of ways. I could create worksheets or project descriptions whose professional appearance can convey to students both the time and energy I put into their instruction. This in turn should reinforce their understanding of the time and energy that I expect from them. More specifically, in a history class there is the possibility of copying and pasting passages from primary sources found on the Internet—such as letters, documents, or journals—onto a document in the program in order to give the source a more appealing appearance. Yellowed and dusty old books may capture my imagination, but that is not always the case for everyone.

Students can reap tremendous benefits as well. Publishing programs, should they be available to all students, present an opportunity to involve students with the subject matter. Students could be given an assignment to create a newsletter, pamphlet, website, or brochure relating to a particular aspect of the curriculum. For units involving political ideologies, for example, students could create a socialist newsletter or a pamphlet designed to persuade American colonists to resist British taxation. World history students could generate a handbook for medieval monasticism. Should they be encouraged to use the Internet to find historical images to add to their creations, they will likely enjoy the occasion to improve their design. All the while they are learning to research historical documents, like photographs. In addition to learning the content in an active and engaging manner, students would be learning or reviewing basic computer skills and increasing their comfort with a variety of programs.

A less obvious benefit of using such applications in student projects is providing for, and encouraging, student creativity. As I created the design for my newsletter, I could see my own personality emerge in its appearance. Very rarely do students have an opportunity to demonstrate their creative abilities on tests and worksheets. Publishing programs both engage students with the material and allow them to apply a personal esthetic to the design. Such freedom is likely to increase a student's enjoyment, and certainly any student is served if he or she can develop positive associations with the subject matter.

Like many skills, computer skills are self-reviewing. In other words, as one continues to learn new programs, previously learned skills are used over and over. Through this process these skills are sharpened to the degree that they can be performed subconsciously, like driving a car. Many of the functions I had learned using word processors, such as copying, pasting, and formatting text and clipart were well practiced in making the newsletter. Technically speaking, most, if not all, operations used were a review. New to me, however, were this software and its applications.

Following is a list of the technology standards for teachers demonstrated in the newsletter:

> NC Basic & Advanced Technology Standards for Teachers demonstrated:
> 1.3 Start an application and create a document
> 1.4 Name, save, retrieve, revise a document
> 1.5 Use printing options
> 1.6 Insert and eject floppy disk and CD-ROM
> 3.1 Word Processing
> 3.2 Copy and move blocks of text
> 3.3 Change text format and style, set margin, line spacing, tabs
> 3.4 Check spelling, grammar, word usage
> 3.5 Create a header or footer

3.6 Insert date, time, page number

3.7 Add columns to document

3.8 Insert clip art into document

8.1 Produce print-based products

8.6 Role of media in effective communication

10.1 Use Computer Skills Curriculum

12.3 Use computers to communicate effectively

National Educational Technology Standards for Teachers demonstrated:

    I. Understanding of Technology Operations and Concepts—A and B

        Click Here to view the standards newsletter

TECHNOLOGY PHILOSOPHY

I resisted our modern technological revolution as long as I could. Despite growing up in a home relatively on the cutting edge in the early 1990s, I learned as little as possible, and what I did I learned with much consternation. I suppose that in those innocent early days I assumed that I was the first person ever to encounter error messages, and my discomfort grew. It wasn't until 1998, my senior year of college, when I was staring down a 50-page thesis requirement that I embraced modern word-processing and the Internet. By this point I had come to realize that we were all learning, all getting error message after error message, and that my organizational tendencies would be well complemented by the capabilities of modern software. So there was the answer. I did not have to be a slave to master Technology. This technology was created by people and for people, and now it was time to harness its power.

Much like that 50-page paper, I now stare down a future in education, where the task of creating a vibrant and effective curriculum seems a nearly endless and impossible one. And like that time three years ago, today I see the potential for technology to serve me as a teacher, my students, and ultimately society at large through a new generation of better-educated, better-informed citizens. What follows is a discussion of my thoughts on how I can use technology to achieve these ends.

The benefits to me as a teacher include the obvious and the not so obvious. My experiences this semester with word processing tools like Microsoft Word and publishing tools like Microsoft Publisher demonstrated the ability to produce attractive and professional worksheets, letters to parents, permission forms, and tests. Beyond their cosmetic advantages, these programs can save tremendous amounts of time and increase communication with parents. Can teachers ever communicate with parents too much? I hope to communicate with parents as often as possible, through these very means, and create materials that convey to students that I am serious about what they are learning.

As demonstrated in the field trip planning experience, other technologies, such as Excel and Access can also be helpful to me as a teacher. Through that project and my own work experience, I have found these programs to be fantastic resources for storing referential information, and will very likely use them to store info about my students. Consider as well the possibilities of a personal web page. If I find it to be useful to my students, I would work to post assignments and helpful resources on my website to help improve communication. Granted, all of these ideas are dependent upon the resources available. Yet even if I only have personal resources available (like a PC), their benefits are certainly worth the price.

Of course, the most important benefit of my increased productivity is (hopefully) a better, more thoughtful and inclusive curriculum for my students. Although many schools are lacking in resources, there will most certainly be computers and other multimedia available to some degree in any high school in the U.S. With these technologies lie the potential to create daily engaging lessons. I am excited by the ability to create graphic organizers in Inspiration; interesting lectures and lecture guides with PowerPoint; and visual aids through DVD, Laserdisc, and VHS. Who knows what else exists to increase the variety of instructional methods? As a thoughtful teacher, I hope to use whatever is available to provide a diverse and engaging environment. Yet the technologies mentioned so far only reach part of the way toward true student engagement.

Students should also be challenged to use new technologies as often as possible, as they provide interesting and active encounters between the student and the material. Depending on the resources available, I hope to have students using software programs for projects I may assign. But this use of software is better used for working with the material, rather than just creating attractive visual aids. I am especially intrigued by the idea of web-based projects, and problem solving through computer applications. This surely requires much planning on my part, but a well-designed project could be an invaluable experience. The greatest value of this active engagement is that it is universal. Some students can learn easily through lectures and bookwork. But all students learn through experience. It is how we all learned to talk, to walk, and interact with our environment. If more teachers can put their students into direct experience with the material, students' learning will likely be more and longer lasting. As a teacher I must use technology to increase these experiential encounters.

This discussion on student use of technology brings me to an important issue, that of safety and ethical use. As with any skill, learners must be guided through their development. No one hands the keys of a car to a fourteen year old without first modeling, then teaching, then guiding. I could even say the same about critical thinking skills. To teach a young person to think independently, but without conscience or personal reflection, can be a dangerous thing. The same is true with modern technology, the Internet in particular. Any use of the Internet in the classroom should be monitored as closely as possible, especially in early years of secondary education. The goal, however, must be to guide students toward independent, responsible, and conscientious use of technology. This is best done, I believe, through modeling this behavior myself, establishing rules about proper use, and then monitoring and gently correcting students' use of the web.

It is rather difficult to foresee exactly what I will, or might, do with technology as a teacher. It depends on too many factors for me to know ahead of time. Indeed, the available resources and curriculum emphases may even change from year to year once I am teaching. Therefore my technology philosophy at this point is necessarily vague. And that philosophy is, essentially, always to design instruction around the learning I want to accomplish, and then use the available resources toward that end. The opposite, looking at the resources and then designing instruction accordingly, is what I want to avoid. With today's technology, regardless of how limited resources may be, the possibilities are nearly endless. With the will, a way will be found.

Home | Standards Newsletter | Technology Standards |
Field Trip Planning | Professional Presentation
Instructional Design Project | Technology Philosophy | Resources

PAUL ROSENBERG
Learning Portfolio
BIS 301, Fall 2001
Arizona State University

TABLE OF CONTENTS

"WHAT A LONG, STRANGE TRIP"
(BIS Autobiography)

When I first came to Arizona State University, I was planning on becoming a business major. I wanted to progress up to a finance major from pre-business. I did not know a great deal about where a finance degree would lead me, but I did know that it could lead me to money, a lot of money, and that was my main objective. As the classes came and went, I realized that I had no interest in finance. I did still have interest in the business aspect of the major, but I was not sure exactly what area. At the time, I was pondering the thought of a communication minor. That was when my advisor suggested to

201

me the Bachelor of Interdisciplinary (BIS) major. At first, I was not sure whether this major would lead me in the right direction, so I decided to think over all of my options. I thought about what I enjoyed. As I reflected on what I was good at and tried to combine my aptitudes with what I also enjoyed, I kept coming to one conclusion. For some strange reason, I actually could say that I enjoyed my time working at Champs. I realized that I was good at selling and at managing, and the best part was that I enjoyed doing both.

Business is still an area I enjoy learning about. My father is an accountant, and I enjoy learning hands-on from him about the finer aspects of business. He has taught me many things about the stock market in which he is a player. I, too, am an investor, though a small one. I subscribe to and read *The Wall Street Journal* daily and follow the rise and fall of the market. As for the communication field, I have just begun taking courses dealing with the various possibilities of communication. There are so many diversified aspects when dealing with communication that gauging my real interests is tough. What I have found most appealing so far is that communication is a discipline that everyone has to deal with on a daily basis, at work, at home, or even just going out with friends.

My goal for the BIS 301 class portfolio is to try to tie my two concentrations of business and communication together and somehow find a way to integrate the areas into a successful job. I have come a long was so far, and there is no turning back. I know that some more mistakes lie ahead in my future, although hopefully not too many. Day by day, my future becomes clearer through my portfolio reflections and my collected materials, and with the combination of the skills that I have already and what I have yet to learn, my future seems to be getting brighter.

Aryana Rousseau
Career Portfolio
Dalhousie University
Spring 2000

Table of Contents

Purpose and Philosophy

This section contains two articles that are very important to my portfolio. The first is my purpose statement explaining why I have developed the portfolio. The second is my philosophy statement giving more insight into who I am, how I think, and what I value.

Writing my purpose and philosophy statements has really encouraged me to think about who I am and what is important to me. Creating the works has helped me to learn more about myself and to gain a better sense of direction in my life.

In the future, I would like to rewrite my purpose and philosophy statements every couple of months in order to rethink my life path and reassess my goals. I know that planning for the future is not something that I can do in one sitting, so I will engage in positive uncertainty. This involves maintaining a positive outlook on life despite uncertainty about the future. I hope that such continual self-reflection will help me find my true course in life.

Purpose Statement

In January 2000, a chain of events led me to take ASSC 1000: Introduction to Career Portfolio at Dalhousie University, a course that deals with career development. The course deals with many of the questions I have been struggling with since my arrival at university: Who am I? Where have I been? What has my past meant to me? Where am I going? The answers, although not yet completely formulated, are a work in progress.

My primary reason for creating a portfolio is self-exploration. Sometimes I ask myself how is it possible that someone not know himself or herself. However, people easily spend their lives without much thought of direction or meaning. Creating my portfolio has given me a reason to break away from this style of living, thinking, and learning. The portfolio has allowed me to take a deeper look at my life and begin to answer questions about myself. My portfolio has forced me to validate and document my activities, instead of allowing me to pass off my accomplishments as "no big deal." Through reflection, I have been able to assess who I was in high school and what it meant to be the person I was. Presently, the portfolio is enabling me to begin looking toward the future. Now that I am in university, I am in charge of my life. I make my own decisions and have the capability to live a wonderful life or an awful one, depending on my choices. To make informed choices about the future, I must know all the available information about myself. My portfolio has allowed me to explore what it is to be me right now and who I want to be in the future.

After collecting the appropriate documents and assembling them in my portfolio, while at the same time attending regular classes in portfolio development and seeing a career counselor, I have ascertained that I have a deep interest in communication on many levels. My interests in writing, theatre, music, dance, and public speaking illustrate my passion. Such interests have also taught me how to listen to what others say, another important aspect of effective communication.

As I have grown, I have recognized the importance of communication in both my personal and my business relationships. I look forward to a career that involves communicating with people to create a sense of understanding. This career, however presently unknown to me, may manifest itself as teaching, writing, journalism, media work, or counseling. In the future, I will modify the purpose of the portfolio and use it as a tool in gaining employment in one of such areas. I hope the portfolio will enable me to provide concrete examples of my work to employers and to prove that I am a talented and dedicated worker.

CHRISTINA TEEL
Learning Portfolio
BIS 301E, Fall 2001
Arizona State University

TABLE OF CONTENTS

SKILLS CHECKLIST

Adapting	Assigning	Compiling	Demonstrating	Empowering
Adjusting	Assisting	Completing	Detailing	Encouraging
Administering	Assuring	Composing	Determining	Enforcing
Advertising	Attaining	Computing	Developing	Estimating
Advising	Bargaining	Consulting	Devising	Evaluating
Analyzing	Briefing	Coordinating	Directing	Examining
Answering	Budgeting	Coping	Discovering	Explaining
Anticipating	Calculating	Copying	Discussing	Expressing
Applying	Checking	Counseling	Displaying	Extracting
Approving	Classifying	Creating	Dissecting	Facilitating
Acquiring	Collaborating	Deciding	Distributing	Filing
Arbitrating	Communicat-	Decorating	Editing	Financing
Arranging	ing	Defining	Eliminating	Gathering
Assessing	Comparing	Delegating	Empathizing	Guiding

Handling	Learning	Preparing	Reinforcing	Summarizing
Helping	Lecturing	Presenting	Relating	Supervising
Hypothesizing	Listening	Printing	Researching	Supplying
Identifying	Managing	Problem-	Reorganizing	Synthesizing
Imagining	Manipulating	solving	Reporting	Talking
Implementing	Mediating	Processing	Navigating	Teaching
Improving	Memorizing	Promoting	Restoring	Team-building
Improvising	Mentoring	Proofreading	Reviewing	Telling
Influencing	Monitoring	Proposing	Revising	Training
Initiating	Motivating	Providing	Risking	Translating
Innovating	Following	Publicizing	Scheduling	Traveling
Inspecting	Observing	Purchasing	Selecting	Treating
Inspiring	Ordering	Reading	Selling	Trouble-
Installing	Organizing	Reasoning	Separating	shooting
Instructing	Participating	Receiving	Serving	Understanding
Integrating	Perceiving	Recommend-	Setting-up	Verbalizing
Interpreting	Performing	ing	Sharing	Visualizing
Interviewing	Persuading	Reconciling	Simplifying	Writing
Inventorying	Pinpointing	Recording	Solving	
Investigating	Planning	Recruiting	Speaking	
Leading	Predicting	Referring	Studying	

SKILLS CHECKLIST REFLECTION

I consider my communication skills my most marketable. I have learned different forms of communication throughout my education in every class I have completed and I fine-tuned these skills in my daily interactions. I have studied the differences in the ways men and women communicate in my Personal Growth and Human Relations class. This was an invaluable class for personal relationships. I find that I have more patience and understanding with my self and others after taking the class. I have studied business communication and communication within groups in small group communication. The interpersonal and intercultural skills I have learned in these classes have strengthened my confidence and presence in business. Whether I am addressing customers or peers, I am more confident in my interactions after taking such courses.

My organizational skills are exemplary. I am a very organized person and through my organizational efforts, I have been able to succeed in school and full-time work. I find that my organizational skills have grown over the years with my responsibilities. One of my strongest skills in this area is time management. I have perfected time management to a fine art. One of my strengths in time management is planning. I do this by beginning and completing projects early so I can review and edit them. I also find myself preparing speeches and presenting them to family and friends to perfect them before speaking in front of my peers, instructors, and employers. The effort I put into time management and organization continually pays off.

I continually work on and improve my leadership skills. I have worked within groups where I have taken a leadership role for classes. I find it easy to organize a project and delegate the duties. I was raised to lead in a manner in which I would want to be led. Always keeping this in mind, I never ask of someone what I am not willing to do myself. I feel that this builds my character with others and that I gain more respect as a leader.

Writing is something I do quite a bit in my education as well as on my job. I am continually working to improve my writing as I feel this is my weakest skill. Although I consider writing as my weakest skill, I list it because I feel that I have made considerable advances in improving this skill. Through my classes, I learn to express myself coherently in words, something I can do much better speaking. I also find myself adapting what I write to the situation.

I have strong experience in team building. I have always worked in a team environment, some positions where I have been a team member and others where I have been a team leader. One of the greatest lessons I have learned in teamwork is to treat everyone as equals. I do not ask something of another that I am not willing to do myself and I feel this is a key to teamwork. I would much rather work as part of a team and accomplish many things than work on my own and accomplish few.

CONNIE THACKABERRY
Honors Portfolio
Kent State University
March 1997

REFLECTION PAPER

Becoming an Actor

Expression. Art. Drama. Theatre. Acting. The scope of expression and the form vary for each individual. Actors from ancient Greeks to current Hollywood favorites have struggled with the process of becoming an actor. For me, much of the struggle down the path towards life as a professional actor has taken place in the last three years of my life. Reflecting on where I was and how far my journey has taken me has allowed me to recognize some of the forces and ideas that have shaped this time of growth for me. The legendary actor Uta Hagen writes about modern-day applications of method acting in her now famous book *Respect for Acting*. She discusses the characteristics a young actor should possess:

> Talent alone is not enough. Character and ethics, a point
> of view about the world in which you live, and an educa-
> tion can and must be acquired and developed. Ideally, the
> young actor should possess or seek a thorough education
> in history, literature, English linguistics, as well as the
> other art forms—music, painting and dance—plus theatre
> history and orientation. (21)

Hagen's statement was so true to me, so real, that without realizing it I took it as my guide. This portfolio has given me the chance once again to reflect on Hagen's words. Both Hagen and my father constantly quote Stanislavsky's favorite line, "Love the art in yourself, not yourself in the art." To me, this means that you should not pursue acting because you have a large ego and want attention, but because it is your vocation. As many actors become distracted by thoughts of fame, they must know what they are searching for at all times. As my mother reminds me, "You just need to keep your eyes on the prize." I guess I have been fortunate to be able to do so.

To me, the prize or the goal is to become a professional actor. For this portfolio, I have chosen works that reflect my interests, my knowledge, and my soul. I want to reflect further on how Hagen's words have shaped my university life. Reflecting on the last three years, I find that my classroom education, my travel in and experience of the world, and my dedication to my art have helped me in becoming an actor.

I first read Hagen's book while in an acting class my freshman year. I took the course mainly because of Dr. Frese, who had been my professor for an honors course the prior semester. I think that she realized I had a great deal of energy and interest in what we were doing in class. Consequently, she always pushed me to give all that I had. I felt that I must have landed in this class for a reason. I knew that I chose it to give my acting some focus and to determine what I needed more work on at that point. But the opportunity to work with Dr. Frese and to learn new acting techniques and theories was invaluable. Hagen's words reassured me that first year that I was doing the right thing in pursuing an English major. Prior to this time, I had realized that I wanted to act but did not want to be stuck in the confines of a university theatre program, acting only in campus productions. For me, English was the most logical choice.

I have always been awed by literature; the texts themselves, especially plays, contain abundant meaning even without the performance. I remember reading *Romeo and Juliet* in my high school freshman English class. I was puzzled when other students had trouble understanding it, even when it was read aloud in class. I was forgetting that I was practically raised on his works. I was taken to my father's acting company rehearsals, and with actors for parents, Shakespeare became material for bedtime stories. I realized that I could not get away from the desire to understand more of the text, more of the language, and to have a chance to examine drama from a literary perspective.

The education part of the last three years has been tied directly to my acting. I think this is the most important aspect of the Hagen quotation. For in order to be an actor, you must be educated. Acting, like every art form, is based only partly on talent. If you have a natural affinity for doing something, it will perhaps be a bit easier for you. But talent alone will not take anyone anywhere. Choosing an English major was not the simplest choice. I was also fascinated by journalism and photography, and I still am. I also liked the idea of becoming a lawyer. I have recently realized that while I adore the idea of "playing" a lawyer or a journalist, I am not as interested in having those careers as I am in the characters themselves. I often wondered, during my first year, if a more traditional undergraduate theatre major would not be more beneficial. I quickly realized that I had the time and freedom to do theatre wherever I wanted. I began acting professionally, working towards my equity card, the summer before I started at Kent State.

I have acted in four other professional productions since then. It was not until last fall that I acted in a show at Kent State.

Choosing the English major was also difficult because compared to the more focused BFA in acting, the English BA required more language, more math, and more science. All of these areas involved studying topics that did not seem so crucial to my acting. Still, I tried to remain focused. When I have to study science notes every night to grasp a concept, or endlessly practice calculus problems, I imagine that I will someday play an astronaut or a calculus professor and that these skills and knowledge will become character resources. I find that I often become interested in ideas and concepts that I never thought I would care about.

In January of my freshman year, I was cast as Cecily Cardew in Oscar Wilde's *The Importance of Being Earnest*. I first read this play when I was ten or 12 and remember adoring Cecily. I thought her so humorous; she pretended things just as I did, only she was practically grown-up. The play turned out as fairy tale-ish as anyone could imagine. Rehearsals were a bit of another story. For the first two weeks, I struggled desperately with the lines, trying to be funny and adorable and sweet all at once and attempting to gain an authentic British accent. It was the first run-through of the play when things finally started clicking. I finally was applying some of the knowledge of both the philosophy material I had read and the textual analysis. I used Zen, method acting techniques I had learned in Dr. Frese's class, and Buber's advice about having an I-Thou relationship. I focused. I studied. And then I let all of this go. By forgetting, by allowing myself just to *do*, something could begin to happen. And it did. My struggle was rewarded because I had chosen to free myself of pressure and to rely on the knowledge that I had within me. . . .

> *"The journey of 1000 miles begins with a single step."*
> *(Lao-Tze)*

There have been many beginning steps on the journey towards becoming an actor. I am sure that steps I took in childhood, steps such as studying Suzuki violin and classical ballet, were activities that drew me closer to my art. My college education was also a beginning step.

The first step that I took by myself in my life journey was the decision to spend last year studying abroad. More recently I have taken another step, perhaps the first major one on the road to becoming an actor. Almost a month ago, I went to Chicago for graduate school auditions. I wish to pursue a Master's of Fine Arts in acting next fall. I was in Chicago to audition for ten professional actor-training programs. Ms. Albers, my acting mentor, told me that this trip was a real beginning for me. She encouraged me to find all the joy I could in it because I had chosen this path for my life. Ms. Albers said that Chicago was the first step in my journey toward life as a professional actor. Then she said that the trip to Chicago was also an extension of my life journey. She pointed out that I'd started it last year when I went to Leicester University as an exchange student and traveled in Europe. I was confused at first. I have acted professionally before. I have already begun earning equity points toward my actor's union card. I just appeared in a professional production at the Cleveland Playhouse. So what could Ms. Albers have meant when she said this?

After Chicago, after all the auditions, I began to realize what she meant. In stepping out of my comfort zone last year, I was able to begin to delve deeper into my own psyche and my own future. Chicago then became a continuation of my journey. My own hopes for the future are clear to me. I, like any other graduate, have many dreams. I have been fortunate enough, as a Kent State student, to have had opportunities to learn in the classroom, to experience life in the vast world around me, and to dedicate a great deal of time to my art form. The combination of all of the artistic, theatrical, literary, and travel experiences has led me to where I am today.

But I also need the chance to continue to grow, to learn, to experience, and to follow those brilliant words of Ms. Hagen. For I know that talent is not enough. I feel that my education, my travels, and my dedication to my art have prepared me for my career. I am certain that in the future, all of the knowledge, insight, and moments of enlightenment I gained here at Kent State will help me to become the actor and person I want to be.

JOSEE VAILLANT
Career Portfolio
Dalhousie University
Spring 2000

TABLE OF CONTENTS

PURPOSE

Experience is the finest teacher in one's journey through life. I believe every-thing happens for a reason and each one of us is put on this earth to fulfill a purpose. My portfolio is a reflection of my experiences and how they have contributed to my strengths and weaknesses along my journey thus far.

My ultimate goal is to become a teacher and this portfolio is a prelimi-nary step toward achieving that goal. It shows how all of my encounters have helped me acquire a clearer picture of what opportunities will most benefit me, in order to shape the course of my future to help me eventually become a successful teacher.

PORTFOLIO PROCESS: A RETROSPECTIVE

What?

When I first heard about creating a portfolio, I was anxious to get started. The concept of having my own portfolio got me excited to get my "stuff" organized. I say "stuff" because that is all I had before I created the portfo-lio—simply different materials scattered and disorganized. The process of creating my portfolio was an interesting journey that led me into personal reflection about my past, present, and planned future. It also gave me a chance to re-examine the theorists we have studied throughout the course.

So What?

When the process first began, I was unsure of being able to create a concrete and complete portfolio, yet I soon discovered differently as I revisited my experiences and how they were of value to me. I was also unsure about the purpose my portfolio was to convey, but this is where my mentors were of help to me: They helped me get focused. After gathering the relevant materials and organizing my sections for them, it was time to evaluate, assess, and analyze what the materials represented to me and how they accurately reflected the purpose of my portfolio. This is what really got me thinking about my future plans. My challenge was no longer about the *what* and the *so what*, but the *now what!* Now that I had realized what my experiences meant to me, it was time to decide how I could apply my new knowledge to my future endeavors.

Now What?

I look back at when I first started creating my portfolio and realize how far I have come. When I first began, the finished product seemed far beyond my reach, and now here it is and I cannot wait to continue building it into a great tool that will of great benefit to me in the future. I am excited about setting goals and adding to my achievements.

I now possess a tool that is essentially a self-portrayal. The purpose of my portfolio will eventually change and help me get into a bachelor of education program. One of the greatest features of a portfolio is that even if it is a finished product, there is no limit to what an individual can continue to bring to it.

JENNIFER WOLF
WEBSITE

Academic | Organizations | Professional

I am currently a Junior at Albion College. My major is Biology with a concentration in Pre-medicine. I also belong to the Honors Institute. This webpage is designed to serve as an interactive portfolio. Each category, academic, organizations and professional, is subdivided into college years.

Freshman Year			
FIRST SEMESTER		SECOND SEMESTER	
Biology 105: Principles of Biology	4.0	Biology 110: Organismal Diversity	3.3
Women's Lives: A Global Perspective	4.0	Chemistry 121: Structure and Equilibrium	4.0
Great Issues in Social Science	4.0	Great Issues in Humanities	4.0
Calculus II	3.0	English Composition	3.7
Marching Band	4.0	Weight Lifting	4.0
		Freshman Seminar in Biology	Pass

Work Experience: Sophomore Year

Company and Position	Responsibilities	Time Frame
Albion College: Computer Lab Assistant	Supervised computer labs, assisted users with computer problems and addressed concerns	August '99–May '00
Albion College: Biology Lab Assistant	Assisted the professor in the teaching of an introductory biology lab, lab preparation and helped students with problems or concerns	January '00–May '00
Albion College: FURSCA research partner	Conducted biological research concerning abnormalities in developing lake trout embryos	May '00–July '00
MMGSC: Camp Health Officer	Supervised a heath center at the Girl Scout camps Innsfree and Metamora. Attended to first aid and health concerns of campers and staff.	July '00–August '00
Pre-Medicine Internships		
Northpointe Pediatrics: Dr. Peter Francis, M.D. General Pediatrician	Observed the operation of a private pediatric practice and witnessed the responsibilities of a pediatrician through participating in office visits and conversation.	A week in May '00
Battle Creek Family Health Center: Dr. Sam Grossman, D.O. General Pediatrician	Observed the operation of a government-funded pediatric practice and witnessed the responsibilities of a pediatrician through participating in office visits and conversation.	June '00–July '00

Recognitions and Awards

Award	Description
Presidential Academic Scholarship	A four year academic scholarship given to high school students with outstanding academic and leadership attributes.
Albion Fellow	A recognition for maintaining a 3.7 GPA for 3 consecutive semesters.
Dean's List—6 semesters	A recognition for maintaining a 3.5 GPA.
Michigan Campus Compact: Commitment to Service Award	The COMMITMENT TO SERVICE award is given to one student per MCC member campus for either the breadth or the depth of her/his community involvement. Recipients, for example, may have devoted multiple years to one program or have demonstrated their leadership by making multiple contributions to her/his institution and community through community service involvement.
Alpha Phi Omega: Service Award	Given to one member a year for outstanding service to chapter, campus and community.

Part IV

Practical Materials

Part IV consists of a wide collection of practical materials—assignment sheets, guidelines, criteria, evaluation rubrics, and other materials—that various individuals and institutions have used as part of developing print and electronic learning portfolios from across disciplines, programs, and types of institutions in higher education.

Albion College, Self-Assessment. A self-assessment guide for students developing digital portfolios, helping them reflect on and write about learning and career or academic goals

Albion College, Four-Year Portfolio Development Plan. Describes the college's four-year portfolio plan, offering students detailed instructions and exercises for developing each year's portion of their digital portfolio

Arizona State University, BIS 301 Portfolio Evaluation Form. Evaluation and scoring rubric for portfolios in an interdisciplinary program course

Arizona State University, BIS 402 Portfolio Evaluation Form. Evaluation and scoring rubric for portfolios in an interdisciplinary program course

Arizona State University, Showcase/Electronic Portfolio Evaluation Form. Evaluation and scoring rubric for electronic portfolios in an interdisciplinary program course

Cape Cod Community College, Math Course Mastery Demonstration Portfolio. Instructions for developing a mastery learning portfolio in a math course

Dalhousie University, Portfolio Reflections. Assignment sheet detailing the purpose and value of portfolio reflections

Kent State University, Honors Senior Portfolio Option, Guidelines and Contract. Contract form and guidelines for developing portfolio

University of Oklahoma, Reflective Writing Assignment, CE 3212: Environmental Engineering I. Instructions for reflection on course content and integration of skills

Saskatchewan University, College of Agriculture, Formulating Learning Objectives. Instructions for portfolio development of reflective statements on experiential learning goals and experiences, linking reflection to specific objectives and means of evaluation

Saskatchewan University, College of Agriculture, Report Guidelines and Sample Questions. Guided exercise for portfolio reflections on experiential work experience

Saskatchewan University, College of Education, Documenting Professional Growth in the Internship: The Professional Portfolio. Instructions for developing a pre-service student teaching portfolio

Self-Assessment

Albion College

EXERCISES

Self-assessment exercises help you examine who you are and where you are headed. Start with one listed below or come up with your own. After completing an exercise, reflect on what you have learned about yourself and how you might apply what you have learned to your goals and plans. You may want to place the exercise and your responses in your portfolio or maybe just your reflection. Since you and your portfolio are ever changing, you are encouraged to revisit the self-assessment stage periodically.

- Discover your interests, abilities, and values.

- Ask yourself why?

- What have you done, what did you learn, and how will you grow?

Discover Your Interests, Abilities, and Values

With the help of DISCOVER, an interactive computer-based self-assessment program available in the student computer labs on campus, you are able to assess your interests, abilities and values and learn how these relate to the world of work. After completing the Interests, Abilities, and Values assessment, reflect on how you responded to the questions and how you can use the outcomes of this assessment as you plan for your future.

Ask Yourself Why?

Why? Getting to where you are right now was based on a series of choices. What was your rationale for making one decision or choice over another? What were the consequences of those decisions?

1) Why did you decide to go to college?

2) Why did you decide to come to Albion College?

3) Why did you decide (or have you not yet decided) to pursue a particular major, concentration, or discipline?

4) Why did you select the courses in which you are currently enrolled?

5) Why did you join your organizations, clubs, and groups?

6) Why do you spend your leisure time the way you do?

Whether this is the first or fourth time completing the Ask Yourself Why assessment, reflect on your responses. What have been the consequences of your decisions? What have been the positive and negative outcomes? How have these decisions impacted other decisions you made, and how will they impact future decisions? How can you use what you have learned about yourself through this assessment as you plan for your future?

What Have You Done, What Did You Learn, and How Will You Grow?

List five experiences you have had and at least one thing you learned from each experience. Identify whether what you learned is a new skill or self-awareness. Write a reflection paragraph on each of these experiences including what led you to the experience, how you can use what you learned now and in the future, and what future experiences you may want to explore or avoid as a result of this experience.

MAKING A PLAN

Where are you, and where are you going? The purpose of your portfolio is to help you bring together your personal, academic, and professional experiences. Self-assessment exercises will help you reflect on how you got to where you are now and where you are going. Goal setting will help you be intentional about how you get where you are going.

During the first year in college, it is very common for the personal, academic, and professional experiences to be separate or loosely connected. Eventually there should be natural links that demonstrate how the three come together. Example: A student who has always been very interested in animals may volunteer at the local Humane Society, work for a veterinarian, and declare a major in biology.

Your academic, personal, and professional plans will serve as the tool or location for sharing the "public" side of your portfolio. Start out by making a paper plan with the headings "Academic," "Personal," and "Professional." Next, jot down topics or concepts that come to mind when you see each heading listed on the page. Finally, decide the topics and concepts that are most important to you and expand on those or highlight why they are important.

Goal Setting

What do you want to do with your life? This is a question high school and college graduates are constantly asked. This question is much easier to answer if broken down into smaller parts. That is what goals are.

How Do I Begin?

1) Start with a long-term or short-term desired outcome. This becomes your **goal statement.**

2) Break your goal statement into smaller parts or steps that describe an action that will contribute to achievement of a goal. These are **objectives.** It is important that your objectives are specific and measurable.

3) To fulfill an objective, you need to have an **action plan.** The action plan is made up of the steps that lead to completion of an objective. It is helpful to include target completion dates in your action plan.

4) Finally, make sure you complete the steps listed on your action plan.

Once you begin to take the steps to achieve your goals you may find out that you need to revise and add to your original objectives and action plan. Set a minimum of three goals followed by a minimum of two objectives, and then the action plan, or the actions that will actually get the objectives accomplished. You might think of your goals in terms of one academic, one personal, and one professional.

Example:

Academic goal:

Go to graduate school to get a Ph.D. in clinical psychology

Objective:

To get an undergraduate major in psychology

To graduate with at least a 3.5 GPA in order to be selective regarding graduate schools

Action Plan:

Speak with the chair of the psychology department to get advice regarding course selection (October)

Speak with my academic advisor about my plan (September)

Set aside time and stick to a study plan (August)

Join Psi Chi, the psychology club (August)

Get help from the writing center whenever I have a paper to write because that is my weakest area academically (as needed)

How to Set S.M.A.R.T. Goals

S— specific. Does your goal provide a direction as well as a means?

M— measurable. How will you measure the progress of your goal?

A— attainable*/active. Is your goal within reasonable reach? Do you provide a means to achieve your goal?

R— realistic*/relevant*. Can your goal be achieved? Does your goal keep you on task?

T— timetable. What is the time frame in which you will achieve your goal?

* *Not necessarily stated in goal—it is something you keep in mind while creating the goal.*

Example of a Smart Goal:

Fall semester 2000 (timetable), I will obtain a GPA above 3.8 by increasing study time through dedication and time management (specific and active). My progress will be measured through set evaluations (measurable).

Four-Year Portfolio Development Plan

Albion College

FIRST-YEAR PORTFOLIO

During your first year, you will be learning the basics of portfolio development. Incorporate what you learn from self-assessment exercises and goal setting to develop academic, personal, and professional plans.

- Self-assessment exercises
- Self-assessment reflection statements
- Academic, personal, and professional goals, objectives, and action plans
- Course schedule
- Student organization membership
- Hobbies
- Interests, abilities, values
- Athletics
- Extracurricular activities
- Volunteer activities
- On- and off-campus jobs
- Portfolio development timeline

- Home or index—Introduce yourself and welcome viewers by telling them a bit about what they can view in your portfolio.
- Academic—Share what you have done and what you plan to do with your course work, highlighting what you learned from your favorite course or project.
- Personal—Share what you are involved in outside the classroom, highlighting an interesting experience.
- Professional—Share some of your professional skills and traits, how you obtained them, and how you use them, highlighting one of which you are especially proud.

SOPHOMORE PORTFOLIO

During your sophomore year, you will be building on the basics. You are at a new stage of development, so reassess who you are with self-assessment exercises. Check up on the goals you set and set new ones. Continue to develop your academic, personal, and professional plans.

- Self-assessment exercises
- Self-assessment reflection statements
- Academic, personal, and professional goals, objectives, and action plans
- Course schedule
- Progress on core coursework
- Student organization membership
- Hobbies
- Interests, abilities, values
- Athletics
- Extracurricular activities
- Volunteer activities
- On- and off-campus jobs
- Leadership opportunities
- Progress toward declared major
- Externships/internships
- Portfolio development timeline

- Home or index—Modify your introduction and welcome if needed.
- Academic—Expand on what you have done and what you plan to do with your course work. Without removing your course or project highlight, share what your major is and how you came to that decision.
- Personal—Expand on what you are involved in outside the classroom. Without removing your highlight of an interesting experience, share how an out of class experience has helped you with your academic or professional development.
- Professional—Expand on some of your professional skills and traits, how you obtained them, and how you use them. Without removing your highlight of a skill or trait that you are especially proud of, share how your choice of a major will impact your professional future.

JUNIOR PORTFOLIO

During your junior year, you can begin to think more about audiences off campus than those on campus. Content is still important, but how you present your information becomes equally important. Since you will most likely not be present when someone views your portfolio, you want to be sure your information flows and is easily found and understood. While you want to make a visual impact, you want to be sure that impact is a positive one.

- Self-assessment exercises
- Self-assessment reflection statements
- Academic, personal, and professional goals, objectives, and action plans
- Course schedule
- Progress on core coursework
- Student organization membership
- Hobbies
- Interests, abilities, values
- Athletics
- Extracurricular activities
- Volunteer activities
- On and off campus jobs
- Leadership opportunities
- Progress toward declared major
- CIS involvement
- Institute involvement
- Writing and research samples
- Portfolio development timeline
- Externships/internships
- Previous briefcase documents

- Home or index—Modify your introduction and welcome if needed.
- Academic—Expand on what you have done and what you plan to do with your course work. You may want to expand on your course or project highlight and what your major is and how you came to that decision. Add a philosophy or mission statement. Highlight involvement in centers for interdisciplinary study and/or institutes. Offer samples of your academic work.
- Personal—After looking at all of the out-of-class experiences you have had, highlight the ones that have had the greatest impact on you. You may want to expand on your highlight of an interesting experience and how an out-of-class experience has helped you with your academic or professional development. Add a philosophy or mission statement.
- Professional—After looking at all of your professional skills and traits, highlight a few that are especially important to your chosen profession. Expand on your reflections regarding your major and the skill or trait of which you are especially proud. Add a philosophy or mission statement and a copy of your résumé.

SENIOR PORTFOLIO

During your senior year, your portfolio is primarily for an off-campus audience. Content is based on who is viewing your portfolio. Since you will most likely not be present when someone views your portfolio, you want to be sure your information flows and is easily found and understood. While you want to make a visual impact, you want to be sure that impact is a positive one.

- Self-assessment exercises
- Self-assessment reflection statements
- Academic, personal, and professional goals, objectives, and action plans
- Course schedule
- Progress on core coursework
- Student organization membership
- Hobbies
- Interests, abilities, values
- Athletics
- Extracurricular activities
- Volunteer activities
- On- and off-campus jobs
- Leadership opportunities
- Progress toward declared major
- CIS involvement
- Institute involvement
- Writing and research samples
- Externships/internships
- Portfolio development timeline
- Previous briefcase documents

- Home or index—Modify your introduction and welcome if needed.
- Academic—Expand on what you have done and what you plan to do with your course work. You may want to expand on your course or project highlight and what your major is and how you came to that decision. Add a philosophy or mission statement. Highlight involvement in centers for interdisciplinary study and/or institutes. Offer samples of your academic work. Highlight involvement in an off-campus program or internship if you participated in one.
- Personal—After looking at all of the out-of-class experiences you have had, highlight the ones that have had the greatest impact on you. You may want to expand on your highlight of an interesting experience and how an out-of-class experience has helped you with your academic or professional development. Develop a philosophy or mission statement.

- Professional—After looking at all of your professional skills and traits, highlight a few that are especially important to your chosen profession. Expand on your reflections regarding your major and the skill/trait of which you are especially proud. Include a philosophy or mission statement and your resume. Highlight involvement in an off-campus program or internship if you participated in one. Reflect on what you are planning for your next step, whether that means graduate school, a job, volunteer work, etc.

BIS 301 Portfolio Evaluation Form Contents Checklist

Arizona State University

REQUIRED (45 POINTS)

- Title page
- Table of contents
- Mission statement
- Autobiography/BIS plan of study and concentration reports
- Skills evaluations lists (3 lists):
    - Career Center Values Checklist
    - Skills Checklist I
    - Skills Checklist II
- Skills learned/developed from courses in emphasis areas
- Skills developed from life/job/internship experiences
    - Indication of where and how you learned each skill
- Personal strengths/weakness inventory list

THREE OF THE FOLLOWING PLUS ONE-PAGE NARRATIVE (10 POINTS)

- Strong Interests Inventory Test/One-page narrative
- Myers-Briggs /Voices of Discovery/One-page narrative
- SIGI/One-page narrative
- Investigating Academic Professional Literature I or II
- Search for integration/interdisciplinary concepts/buzz words
- BIS résumé/path to dream job

EXTRA (5 POINTS)

- Résumé
- Writing sample (with favorable evaluations if possible)
- Academic accomplishments within areas of emphasis
- Letters of recommendation
- Academic transcript
- Awards or certificate of merit or accomplishment
- Samples of artwork/design/project
- Write-up/evidence of volunteer activity
- Other

APPEARANCE (40 POINTS)

Materials:

- Attractive, appropriate binder
- Plastic sheets/page covers
- Dividers

___Excellent ___Very Good ___Fair ___Needs Improvement ___No Effort Made

Neatness:

___Excellent ___Very Good ___Fair ___Needs Improvement ___No Effort Made

Organization:

___Excellent ___Very Good ___Fair ___Needs Improvement ___No Effort Made

Creativity:

___Excellent ___Very Good ___Fair ___Needs Improvement ___No Effort Made

Overall Effort:

___Excellent ___Very Good ___Fair ___Needs Improvement ___No Effort Made

BIS 402 Portfolio Evaluation Form Contents Checklist

Arizona State University

REQUIRED (45 POINTS)

- Title page
- Table of contents
- Mission statement
    - ~ Autobiography/personal statement
    - ~ DOG/DARS
    - ~ BIS plan of study/list of courses (if applicable)
- BIS Section:
    - ~ Copy of BIS page
    - ~ Sample of interdisciplinary work in 301
    - ~ Career research (informational interview?)
    - ~ Other relevant work in 301, syllabus (?)
    - ~ 302 work (?)
- 401 section:
    - ~ Description of experience (copy of 402 web page?)
    - ~ Time logs, midterm, final paper
- 402 section:
    - ~ Syllabus/literature review/critical analysis interdisciplinary paper
- Skills:
    - ~ Strength/weakness personal inventory
    - ~ Skills learned/developed from courses in emphasis areas

- Skills developed from life/job/internship experiences
- Indication of where and how you learned each skill

Extra (5 points)

- Résumé
- Writing sample (with favorable evaluations if possible)
- Academic accomplishments within areas of emphasis
- Letters of recommendation
- Academic transcript/DARS report
- Awards or certificate of merit or accomplishment
- Samples of artwork/design/project
- Write-up/evidence of volunteer activity
- Other

Appearance (50 points)

Materials:

- Attractive, appropriate binder
- Plastic sheets/page covers
- Dividers

___Excellent ___Very Good ___Fair ___Needs Improvement ___No Effort Made

Neatness:

___Excellent ___Very Good ___Fair ___Needs Improvement ___No Effort Made

Organization:

___Excellent ___Very Good ___Fair ___Needs Improvement ___No Effort Made

Creativity:

___Excellent ___Very Good ___Fair ___Needs Improvement ___No Effort Made

Overall Effort:

___Excellent ___Very Good ___Fair ___Needs Improvement ___No Effort Made

Showcase/Electronic Portfolio Evaluation Form

Arizona State University

CONTENT

- Title page
- Table of contents
- Mission statement
- BIS web page
- Sample work
- Internship experience
- Work experience
- Résumé
- Skills
- Reference letters
- Sample work

1) Portfolio statement clearly answers the question, "How do I want prospective employers to think of me and my work?"

   YES!   Yes   Average   no   NO!

2) Selection: Do the artifacts in your showcase portfolio represent your qualifications for the position?

   YES!   Yes   Average   no   NO!

3) Interdisciplinarity/Synthesis/Integration: Did you represent your interdisciplinary education adequately? Did you include evidence of inter-

disciplinary work? Did you indicate that you have done interdisciplinary work/research/projects?

YES!   Yes   Average   no   NO!

4) Language Mechanics: Is your portfolio free of spelling, punctuation, and grammatical errors?

YES!   Yes   Average   no   NO!

5) Organization: Is your showcase portfolio appropriately organized?

YES!   Yes   Average   no   NO!

DESIGN

Typography: Treatment of font size and style support your design.
Balance of design: White space, centered, graphic/picture placement.
Consistency of design: Reader can access work easily; consistent page layout.
Conciseness: No extra artifacts that don't support your message.

___Excellent ___Very Good ___Fair ___Needs Improvement ___No Effort Made

APPEARANCE

Professional quality: Easily accessible, attractive, and appropriate.
Materials: Binder, dividers/plastic sheets.

___Excellent ___Very Good ___Fair ___Needs Improvement ___No Effort Made

Creativity:

___Excellent ___Very Good ___Fair ___Needs Improvement ___No Effort Made

Self-Representation:

___Excellent ___Very Good ___Fair ___Needs Improvement ___No Effort Made

Overall Effort:

___Excellent ___Very Good ___Fair ___Needs Improvement ___No Effort Made

Math Course Mastery Demonstration Portfolio

Cape Cod Community College

In order to demonstrate that we have mastered the material presented in Chapters 11, 12, and 14 (time permitting), we are going to develop a mastery portfolio. This will include enough materials to prove that you know the content required. You might wish to show your portfolio to a fellow student in the class to obtain feedback or show it to some one outside of the class. Then you should edit the portfolio by adding more material or deleting items that are not helpful to the assessment process.

SUGGESTIONS FOR INFORMATION TO BE INCLUDED IN THE PORTFOLIO

- Anything you feel will show me that you understand how to do the operations described in the chapter section. Use your discretion but leave no stone unturned.

- Completed problems from the exercises at the end of each section.

- Problems worked out in class on worksheets or in groups, presented in legible form.

- Copies of your 3x5 flashcards or notes.

- Your written summary of each chapter section if that is what you use from which to study.

- Materials gleaned from the math lab or obtained from getting tutoring help.

- Sample mastery demonstrations completed as take-home exercises.

What have I left out that will help me determine whether you have learned the material under consideration?

[Available: http://home.capecod.net/~tpanitz/ewacbook/ch12.html]

Portfolio Reflections

Dalhousie University

Each of the required five sections of your portfolio must contain some introductory statements explaining why you have chosen to include these artifacts or documents, how they relate to the purpose of your portfolio, and how they relate to the career development theory we have studied.

Your portfolio will be assessed at three levels of critical reflection. As MacIsaac and Jackson (1994) explain, the most elementary reflections include simple labels, descriptions, etc. As they describe in their article (in your reading package), at this level you are simply *remembering the what, when, and how.*

The next level demands that you move beyond the remembering stage and demonstrate how you analyze, interrelate, and synthesize your materials. At this level, you are *reflecting on the meaning* your section has for you.

At the highest level of reflection, you are not only remembering and reflecting on the meaning of your materials and experiences but also *discussing your future*—the next steps in your learning. At each level of reflection, it is important for you to think about and discuss your gap analysis. *A gap analysis* is simply a reflection on what you have yet to learn as it relates to your section and your purpose statement. It could be that you've identified weak areas that you plan to improve or knowledge gaps that you plan to overcome. *When these reflective comments also reference and integrate personally relevant career development theories, you are demonstrating mastery of the material.*

When introducing your sections for the purposes of this course, or to any audience interested in your learning and personal reflection, you may find it helpful to frame your commentary as "*... this is what I've learned from ... AND ... this is what I'll do with what I've learned ...*" Your reflective commentaries are best when they answer each of these three questions:

1) What?

2) So what?

3) Now what?

The answers to these questions reflect the experiential learning model of your classes and labs.

See me for consultation about the depth of your reflections, privacy issues, the use of your reflections as they relate to interview preparation, and how to edit your portfolio to use in your job search. Remember the marking matrix is available for your review prior to your submission.

Jeanette Hung (1999). Dalhousie Career Portfolio 494-7074 or Dalhousie Counselling Services 494-2081.

MacIsaac, D., & Jackson, L. (1994). Assessment processes and outcomes: Portfolio construction. *New Directions for Adult and Continuing Education, 62,* 63–72.

Honors Senior Portfolio Option, Guidelines, and Contract

Kent Sate University

Professor and Student: Please read the guidelines on the back of this sheet. This completed form must be returned to the honors office for approval as indicated. The student will then be registered for one credit hour (HONR 40085).

CONTRACT

This completed contract must be submitted to the Honors College by the end of the first week of classes during the semester in which the portfolio project is to be completed.

_____Semester, 20____

_____   _____
(Student's name)   I.D. Number

_____   _____
(Address)   (Phone No.)

    As described in the guidelines on the back of this sheet, this project involves the selection, editing, and preparation in final form of a collection (approximately eight to ten artifacts) of work from the past four years; a 15- to 25-page reflective paper that explains how each artifact contributed to the student's intellectual and/or personal growth; and an exit interview.

_____   _____
Signature of student   Signature of professor

_____   _____
Signature of honors advisor   Professor (please print)

_____   _____
Department   Date

_____   _____
Dean, Honors College   Date

During the first two weeks of the semester, the student, the professor, and the Senior Portfolio Review Committee should meet to discuss the details and expectations for the portfolio project. The student should contact the portfolio program coordinator in the Honors College at x 2312 to arrange this meeting.

for Honors College use only
Initial meeting date_____   Exit interview date_____

*   *   *   *   *

GUIDELINES FOR THE HONORS SENIOR PORTFOLIO

Introduction

The senior portfolio provides an opportunity for students to review their work from the past four years and to select from that work eight to ten artifacts that provide the best evidence of meeting the following Honors College goals: academic excellence, campus and community service, global awareness, appreciation of cultural events and institutions, and personal growth.

The portfolio will consist of two parts: 1) documentation of these carefully selected milestones over the past four years in the context of Honors College goals, and 2) a reflective paper which integrates this collection with current personal observations of educational growth and development. The documentation may take many forms (e.g., outstanding papers, supervisor's letters, taped work, journal entries, brief response papers to cultural events attended). The reflective paper should be 15 to 25 pages long and should interpret the college experience as represented by the documents. The portfolio will conclude with an exit interview.

The student must receive written permission (see form on reserve side) from the instructor under whose guidance the portfolio collection and paper will be completed and who will chair the exit interview. The instructor will be responsible for grading this one-credit-hour project.

Student's Responsibilities

The portfolio collection should include examples of work drawn from across the four years that represent meaningful experiences as they relate to such Honors College values as are listed above. The eight to ten artifacts in the collection may include written, visual, and taped entries. Specific suggestions for possible portfolio collection pieces include the following: an outstanding colloquium paper, a brief reaction paper to a cultural event, and samples of work which are sources of particular pride or which represent significant growth. Summary narratives describing special learning experiences and evaluations from supervisors of relevant volunteer or learning activities are also appropriate. An annotated listing of extracurricular activities which describes campus and community service and any awards received is also acceptable.

The 15- to 25-page reflective paper by its very title suggests that this essay will contain highly subjective and personal material. In this overview and critical analysis of four years of individual experiences as an honors student at KSU, the challenge is to integrate a collection of outstanding work with a carefully considered evaluation of academic and personal growth. The portfolio is a retrospective effort to make meaning of the student's college career.

The student will provide three draft copies of the portfolio to the Honors College one week prior to the exit interview. The student may choose to submit a final copy to the Honors College. Upon completion of the portfolio, the student will be asked to submit a short (one-paragraph) summary of the experience for the *On Our Own* publication.

The completed contract on the reverse side must be submitted to the Honors College by the end of the first week of classes during the semester in which the portfolio project is to be completed.

Faculty Advisor's Role

The faculty portfolio advisor will be selected by the student and typically will be someone familiar with the student's best academic work. Ideally, the advisor will also know and be interested in the student's more general educational goals and activities. The portfolio advisor will help the student determine the specific goals of the project, review the items for the final collection, discuss the physical layout of the portfolio, help identify themes and directions of the work, discuss how to integrate the reflective paper with the collected documentary work, and review drafts of the reflective paper.

The faculty advisor will be responsible for grading the one-credit-hour portfolio and should plan regular meetings with the student to assess progress, ask probing questions, and offer guidance. The faculty advisor should also plan to attend the initial meeting as well as chair the exit interview. At any point during the process, the faculty advisor should feel free to contact the portfolio coordinator in the Honors College with any questions or concerns. The advisor should also keep a copy of these guidelines for reference.

Honors College Role

Upon receipt of the completed form (by the end of the first week of the semester), the Honors College will register the student for HONR 40085. An initial meeting will be scheduled with the student, the faculty advisor, and the Senior Portfolio Review Committee during the first two weeks of the semester to answer any questions and provide any details about the project that are not apparent in these guidelines. Sample portfolios will be available at this meeting. The Senior Portfolio Review Committee consists of the student's honors advisor and the honors portfolio coordinator, with an invitation to the honors dean. The portfolio coordinator will be available during the semester to answer any questions the student and/or faculty advisor may have about the portfolio guidelines.

The exit interview will be scheduled for sometime before the 12th week of the semester. The exit interview will also include the student and the Senior Portfolio Review Committee. The Honors College will reimburse the student for the three copies required at this interview. The Senior Portfolio Review Committee may make suggestions regarding the compiling, editing, and presentation of the final portfolio.

Honors Portfolio Coordinator: Vicki Bocchicchio, x 2312

CE 3212: Environmental Engineering I Reflective Writing Assignment (Learning Portfolio)

University of Oklahoma

Reflective writing activities can range from simple one or two sentence thoughts taken at the end of a lecture or assignment (the "one-minute paper"), to running commentary throughout the course (the learning log or diary), to a synthesis document prepared at the end of a major topic or at the end of the semester (the learning portfolio). In this course, we will use a variation of each type.

Implementation

Starting with the section of the course devoted to water distribution systems, we will begin an experiment with reflective writing. At the end of every other week, we will ask each student to visit the class web site and write a short paragraph (one to five sentences) in which you reflect on the past week's activities. These will be read only by the faculty, who will provide some feedback. (This will also help us gauge the effectiveness of our classroom activities.) When writing, consider such questions as:

- What is the most important concept that you learned since the previous reflection?

- What is the relationship of this material to other topics?

- What material do you understand the least?

- What gaps do you see in the material?

- How do you feel about open-ended design problems?

- Do you understand how to use the software as an analysis and design tool, and do you recognize its limitations?

- Do you feel comfortable identifying an approach to a problem and making good engineering assumptions?

At the end of each major topical section in the course, we will ask you to prepare a one-page essay. In preparing this essay, students will consider three aspects of learning—content, context, and process—by addressing these three questions, respectively:

- What have you learned about the topic?

- How does this learning fit into your life's goals (professional and personal)?

- What have you learned about how to learn, particularly as the process of learning relates to open-ended design questions?

For this essay, we encourage you to look back over your weekly reflections and synthesize these thoughts and any new ones into a coherent statement. Please prepare your essay with your favorite word processor and then cut and paste it into the form dialogue box on the web. We encourage you to circulate your drafts among your peers in order to get feedback. In fact, you will probably be surprised that others share similar concerns and frustrations about the course or material.

Since we are starting this process a little late, we would also like you to prepare a two-part essay that looks back at the first part of the course (that is, the material that formed the basis for homework 1, 2, and 3). The first part will be reflective in nature, as described in the second paragraph of this "Implementation" section. Be sure to comment on what things you have learned well (and why) and what things you do not feel you learned well (and why). The second part should be more substantive in nature; it should comment on how the topics that formed the basis of the homework assignments are part of an integrated whole. This midterm essay should be about one to three pages in length and submitted via the web, as instructed above.

At the end of the semester, we would like you to pull the midterm and topical essays together into a single document that reflects on the entire course. In preparing this document (three to five pages), consider the following questions:

- What key ideas or information have you learned about water resources engineering?

- What have you learned about how to use or apply the technical content of this course?

- In what areas do you have the most and least confidence? Why do you suppose this is the case?

- What have you been able to integrate, within or external to this course?

- What have you learned about the human dimension of the subject, regarding yourself and/or your interaction with others?

- What new interests or valuing (that is, the importance of the topic relative to your past experiences) have you acquired as a result of this learning experience?

- What did you learn about yourself as a problem solver?

- What have you learned about how to learn?

This final document should be bound together with your homework assignments to form a completed learning portfolio for the course.

Grading

Only the midterm and final essays will be assigned a letter grade. The grade will be based on the depth of your reflection and not the depth of your understanding of the technical material (the latter will be covered by the homework scores and the final exam). We expect your essay to be grammatically correct and thus readable, although we will not significantly penalize you for minor grammatical mistakes.

Formulating Learning Objectives (Instructions)

University of Saskatchewan, College of Agriculture

Learning objectives are written from your point of view and focus on your intent to learn. You should develop four to seven objectives for each work term, based on both personal and professional goals to cover activities such as routine duties, problem solving activities, new skills and accomplishments, personal improvement, and creative opportunities. You may find that at the beginning of the work term the objectives are quite general; however, after a week or two at the job, they should be much more specific and answer the following questions:

- *What* is the task to be accomplished?
- *How* will I carry out the task?
- *When* will it be completed?
- *How and by whom* will it be evaluated?

Statement of Objectives

I have met with my supervisor and have set the following objectives for my four-month work term. We have also discussed the assessment procedures to determine if I am meeting my objectives.

Objective	Means of Evaluation
	I will know I have achieved this objective when:

Report Guidelines
(Sample Questions)

University of Saskatchewan, College of Agriculture

The following questions are meant as an outline to guide you in your reflection about the work experience and what you learned. For each, consider and describe the source of the learning—employer, colleagues, self, clients, others.

Give a detailed description of the significant work you did and why. Compare two days or weeks at your job—one from the beginning of your placement and one from the end:

- How did you progress both in terms of the quality and quantity of the work you did?

- How did your confidence grow?

Explain what you learned about the employer:

- Who are its suppliers, customers, clients, competitors?

- What is its place in the industry or larger context of agriculture in Saskatchewan, Canada, the world?

- How did the working environment affect your learning?

- What type of company is it: multinational, family-owned, government?

- What is the company structure: lines of authority, hierarchy?

- Did you experience any conflicts in the workplace and what did you learn from the way they were handled?

Everyone learns from mistakes, trial and error, or practice:

- What did you learn in this way?

- Were your colleagues and supervisors supportive and tolerant of you as you learned?

- How did the feedback you received assist in your professional and personal development?

Describe how your work experience and your classroom learning complemented one another.

- How well did your university courses prepare you for the workplace?

- How will the work experience fit into your future university learning?

Describe what you learned about work:

- Do you prefer to work independently, as a team member, etc.?

- How many interactions do you like with the public? Do you prefer office/lab work or meeting customers and clients regularly?

- Do you enjoy/feel confident about giving advice and suggestions to supervisors, colleagues, clients?

Documenting Professional Growth in the Internship: The Professional Portfolio

University of Saskatchewan, College of Education

The process of portfolio development recommended by the Centre for School-Based Experiences, College of Education, is "Project, collect, select, reflect."

1) Project

Compose a statement of your philosophy of education. This will help you to define your nature as a teacher. Clarifying your vision of yourself as teacher will enable you to identify what you want your portfolio to show about you to prospective employers. The planning of a portfolio can be likened to lesson planning: you begin with the objectives: what do I want the portfolio to show about me? Then you plan the content to convey that message.

2) Collect

Begin to identify artifacts which will illustrate those qualities you want to document in the portfolio. Working from the qualities to the artifacts will help to produce a more creative and accurate portrait of you. If you don't have available an artifact which illustrates a particular attribute, you can make plans to generate one.

3) Select

As you choose items to include, remember portfolios are representative, not comprehensive. Each artifact chosen should represent at least one significant aspect of you and/or your teaching. The audience of your portfolio, especially prospective employers, will have limited time to review its contents, so you want to select with care those items which will be most effective in presenting your strengths.

4) Reflect

We recommend that each artifact be accompanied by a description of the context and a rationale for including that piece. This commentary should reflect on the teaching and learning documented, elaborating and interpreting the portfolio entry. Explain why this artifact was chosen and describe how this artifact illustrates your growth in a particular teaching skill. In other words, what does this entry demonstrate about you and your teaching? What does it show about your professional growth? How does it illustrate the effect of your teaching on your pupils? (http://www.usask.ca/education/csbe/portfolio.htm)

References

Annis (Ferrill), L., & Jones, C. (1995). Student portfolios: Their objectives, development, and use. In P. Seldin & Associates, *Improving college teaching* (pp. 181–190). Bolton, MA: Anker.

Arter, J. A., & Spandel, V. (1992). NCME instructional module: Using portfolios of student work in instruction and assessment. *Educational Measurement: Issues and Practice, 11* (1), 36–44.

Barrett, H. (2000a). Create your own electronic portfolio: Using off-the-shelf software to showcase your own or student work. *Learning & Leading with Technology.* Retrieved from http://www.electronicport folios.com/portfolios/iste2k.html

Barrett, H. (2000b). Electronic portfolios = multimedia development + portfolio development. Retrieved from http://transition.alaska.edu/ www/portfolios/EPDevProcess.html#eval

Barrett, H. (2000c). Using Adobe Acrobat for electronic portfolio development. *Association for the Advancement of Computing in Education.* Retrieved from http://www.electronicportfolios.com/portfolios/site paper2001.html

Bean, J. C. (1996). *Engaging ideas: The professor's guide to integrating writing, critical thinking, and active learning in the classroom.* San Francisco, CA: Jossey-Bass.

Black, B. (1998). Using the SGID method for a variety of purposes. *To Improve the Academy: Vol. 17. Resources for Faculty, Instructional, and Organizational Development* (pp. 245–262). Stillwater, OK: New Forums Press.

Bloom, B. S. (Ed.). (1956). *Taxonomy of educational objectives: The classification of educational goals:* Volume 1, *Cognitive domain.* New York, NY: McKay.

Brookfield, S. D. (1995). *Becoming a critically reflective teacher.* San Francisco, CA: Jossey-Bass.

Bruffee, K. A. (1993). *Collaborative learning: Higher education, interdependence, and the authority of knowledge.* Baltimore, MD: Johns Hopkins University Press.

Burch, C. B. (1997). Finding out what's in their heads: Using teaching portfolios to assess English education students—and programs. In K. B. Yancey & I. Weiser (Eds.), *Situating portfolios: Four perspectives* (pp. 263–277). Logan, UT: Utah State University Press.

Cambridge, B. L. (Ed.). (2001). *Electronic portfolios: Emerging practices in student, faculty, and institutional learning.* Washington, DC: American Association for Higher Education.

Campbell, D. M., Cignetti, P. B., Melenyzer, B. J., Nettles, D. H., & Wyman, R. M., Jr. (2001). *How to develop a professional portfolio: A manual for teachers* (2nd ed.). Boston, MA: Allyn and Bacon.

Campbell, D. M., Melenyzer, B. J., Nettles, D. H., & Wyman, R. M., Jr. (2000). *Portfolio and performance assessment in teacher education.* Boston, MA: Allyn and Bacon.

Claywell, G. (2001). *The Allyn and Bacon guide to writing portfolios.* Boston, MA: Allyn and Bacon.

D'Aoust, C. (1992). Portfolios: Process for students and teachers. In K. B. Yancey (Ed.), *Portfolios in the writing classroom: An introduction* (pp. 39–48). Urbana, IL: National Council of Teachers of English.

Dewey, J. (1910). *How we think.* Boston, MA: D. C. Heath.

Edgerton, R., Hutchings, P., & Quinlan, K. (1991). *The teaching portfolio: Capturing the scholarship in teaching.* Washington, DC: American Association for Higher Education.

Emig, J. A. (1971). *The composing processes of twelfth graders* (NCTE Research Report No. 13). Urbana, IL: National Council of Teachers of English.

Emig, J. A. (1977). Writing as a model of learning. *College Composition and Communication, 28,* 122–128.

Fink, L. D. (2001). Higher-level learning: The first step toward more significant learning. *To Improve the Academy: Vol. 19. Resources for Faculty, Instructional, and Organizational Development* (pp. 113–130). Bolton, MA: Anker.

Fink, L. D. (2003). *Designing courses for significant student learning: Making dreams come true.* San Francisco, CA: Jossey-Bass.

Gordon, R. (1994). Keeping students at the center: Portfolio assessment at the college level. *Journal of Experiential Education, 17* (1), 23–27.

Hayes, J. R., & Flower, L. S. (1980). Identifying the organization of writing processes and the dynamics of composing: Making plans and juggling constraints. In L. W. Gregg & E. R. Steinbert (Eds.), *Cognitive processes in writing* (pp. 3–50). Hillsdale, NJ: Lawrence Erlbaum Associates.

Hillocks, G., Jr. (1995). *Teaching writing as reflective practice: Integrating theories.* Language and Literacy Series. New York, NY: Teachers College Press.

Hutchings, P. (1990). Learning over time: Portfolio assessment. *AAHE Bulletin, 42* (8), 6–8.

Hutchings, P. (Ed.). (1998). *The course portfolio: How faculty can examine their teaching to advance practice and improve student learning.* Washington, DC: American Association for Higher Education.

Kaufman, C., & Jafari, A. (2002, March 26). What is an electronic portfolio? Retrieved from http://www.eportconsortium.org/old/whatis.aspx

Kimball, M. A. (2003). *The web portfolio guide: Creating electronic porfolios for the web.* New York, NY: Longman.

Kolb, D. (1984). *Experiential learning as the science of learning and development.* Englewood Cliffs, NJ: Prentice-Hall.

Lankes, A. M. D. (1995). *Electronic portfolios: A new idea in assessment.* Syracuse, NY: ERIC Clearinghouse on Information & Technology. (ERIC Document Reproduction Service No. ED390377)

Lindemann, E. (1982). *A rhetoric for writing teachers.* New York, NY: Oxford University Press.

Martin-Kniep, G. O. (1999). *Capturing the wisdom of practice: Professional portfolios for educators.* Alexandria, VA: Association for Supervision and Curriculum Development.

Moon, J. (1999). *Learning journals: A handbook for academics, students and professional development.* London, England: Kogan Page.

Murphy, S. (1997). Teachers and students: Reclaiming assessment via portfolios. In K. B. Yancey & I. Weiser (Eds.). *Situating portfolios: Four perspectives* (pp. 72–88). Logan, UT: Utah State University Press.

Murray, J. P. (1995). *Successful faculty development and evaluation: The complete teaching portfolio* (ASHE-ERIC Higher Education Report No. 8). Washington, DC: George Washington University.

National Education Association. (2000–2001). *Technology and portfolio assessment.* Retrieved from http://www.nea.org/bt/5-profession/5-3-nres.html

Perry, M. (1997). Producing purposeful portfolios. In K. B. Yancey & I. Weiser (Eds.), *Situating portfolios: Four perspectives* (pp. 182–189). Logan, UT: Utah State University Press.

Schön, D. (1983). *The reflective practitioner: How professionals think in action.* New York, NY: Basic Books.

Schön, D. (1987). *Educating the reflective practitioner: Toward a new design for teaching and learning in the professions.* San Francisco, CA: Jossey-Bass.

Seldin, P., & Associates. (1993). *Successful Use of Teaching Portfolios.* Bolton, MA: Anker.

Seldin, P. (1997). *The teaching portfolio: A practical guide to improved performance and promotion/tenure decisions* (2nd ed.). Bolton, MA: Anker.

Seldin, P., Annis (Ferrill), L., & Zubizarreta, J. (1995). Answers to common questions about the teaching portfolio. *Journal on Excellence in College Teaching, 6* (1), 57–64.

Shore, B. M., et al. (1986). *The teaching dossier* (revised ed.). Ottawa, ON: Canadian Association of University Teachers.

Springfield, E. (2001). A major redesign of the Kalamazoo portfolio. In B. L. Cambridge (Ed.), *Electronic portfolios: Emerging practices in student, faculty, and institutional learning* (pp. 53–59). Washington, DC: American Association for Higher Education.

Sunstein, B. S. (2000). Be reflective, be reflexive, and beware: Innocent forgery for inauthentic assessment. In B. S. Sunstein & J. H. Lovell (Eds.), *The portfolio standard: How students can show us what they know and are able to do* (pp. 3–14). Portsmouth, NH: Heinemann.

Weiser, I. (1997). Revising our practices: How portfolios help teachers learn. In K. B. Yancey & I. Weiser (Eds.), *Situating portfolios: Four perspectives* (pp. 293–301). Logan, UT: Utah State University Press.

Williams, J. D. (2000). Identity and reliability in portfolio assessment. In B. S. Sunstein & J. H. Lovell (Eds.), *The portfolio standard: How students can show us what they know and are able to do* (pp. 135–148). Portsmouth, NH: Heinemann.

Wright, W. A., & Barton, B. (2001). Students mentoring students in portfolio development. In J. E. Miller, J. E. Groccia, & M. S. Miller (Eds.), *Student-assisted teaching: A guide to faculty-student teamwork* (pp. 69–76). Bolton, MA: Anker.

Wright, W. A., Knight, P. T., & Pomerleau, N. (1999). Portfolio people: Teaching and learning dossiers and innovation in higher education. *Innovative Higher Education, 24* (2), 89–103.

Yancey, K. B. (1997). Teacher portfolios: Lessons in resistance, readiness, and reflection. In K. B. Yancey & I. Weiser (Eds.), *Situating portfolios: Four perspectives* (pp. 244–262). Logan,, UT: Utah State University Press.

Yancey, K. B. (2001). Digitized student portfolios. In B. L. Cambridge (Ed.), *Electronic portfolios: Emerging practices in student, faculty, and institutional learning* (pp. 15–30). Washington, DC: American Association for Higher Education.

Young, J. R. (2002, March 8). "E-Portfolios" could give students a new sense of their accomplishments. *The Chronicle of Higher Education,* pp. A31–A32.

Zubizarreta, J. (1994). Teaching portfolios and the beginning teacher. *Phi Delta Kappan, 76* (4), 323–326.

Zubizarreta, J. (1995). Using teaching portfolio strategies to improve course instruction. In P. Seldin & Associates, *Improving college teaching* (pp. 167–179). Bolton, MA: Anker.

Zubizarreta, J. (1997). Improving teaching through teaching portfolio revisions: A context and case for reflective practice. In J. K. Roth (Ed.), *Inspiring teaching: Carnegie professors of the year speak* (pp. 123–133). Bolton, MA: Anker.

Zubizarreta, J. (1999). Evaluating teaching through portfolios. In P. Seldin & Associates, *Changing practices in evaluating teaching: A practical guide to improved faculty performance and promotion/tenure decisions* (pp. 162–182). Bolton, MA: Anker.

Index